What Others Are Saying About
Mimi, Money and Me

"Davis is a brilliant classroom teacher and she brings that same skill to her writing, using humor to debunk common myths, making her points with real-life stories, and explaining legal obligations with clarity. With this book, Davis gives readers the tools they need to take charge of their financial lives. It should be read cover to cover and kept close by as a reference book. It is a valuable primer for all ages."
Teresa Schwartz, attorney, former Deputy Director, Federal Trade Commission; Washington, DC

"When reading "*Mimi, Money and Me*," I felt like I was a "fly on the wall" listening to a mother explaining to her children the ins and outs of how to use money; or, sitting in on a conversation among a group of girlfriends asking questions, some of which were personal, and sharing their own stories about how money had impacted their lives. The book speaks to those audiences and so many others about the common sense as well as complex issues we face daily in managing money. I can't wait to give a copy to my children and my friends! It should be a must read for school and college students as a primer for learning to plan their financial futures, and for learning to avoid many of the "pitfalls" that so many of them have faced and spend a long time trying to correct! Kudos to Patricia and Mimi for taking the mystery out of financial planning and management and for doing it in such an enjoyable way!"
Dr. Barbara Anderson, former Assistant Commissioner, New Jersey Public Schools; New Jersey

"*... Mimi, Money and Me*" is a refreshing approach to helping people understand some of the little things about money that can cause them BIG financial headaches. Davis' book helps you make sure your reality is always based on the right information. Information is the true source of power and this book gives it to you in 101 easy-to-swallow bits."

Elisabeth Donati, author, presenter, entrepreneur, Creative Wealth International; Santa Barbara, CA

"... a must read for anyone trying to get onto the road to financial freedom. Written in a delightful, easy-to-read format, "*Mimi, Money and Me*" is enlightening, witty, practical, informational and beneficial to people of all ages. It gives you the financial savvy to make smart decisions about your money."

Retired LTC William Dexter, Deputy Director, IDEA Public Charter School; Washington, DC

"I had the privilege of knowing the real Mimi for many years. Her wit, humor and knowledge were dispensed in a lighthearted, no nonsense way. She would be pleased that so many of us will get to share her words of wisdom. In *Mimi, Money and Me*, Patricia Davis uses that same no-nonsense, practical, direct and informative way to teach us how to play the money game, to win. It is a primer for all, from young adults to seniors. As an educator, I think this book is a must read for anyone who wants to enjoy the benefits of a life of financial freedom."

Mischelle Johnson, retired educator, Washington, DC Public Schools; Washington, DC

Mimi, Money and Me

101 Realities About Money Daddy Never Taught Me

But Mama Always Knew

By

Patricia A. Davis

Your Personal GPS As You Travel the Road to Financial Freedom

Mimi, Money and Me
101 Realities About Money Daddy Never Taught Me
But Mama Always Knew

Published by Davis Financial Services
Design by Pickett Signs Publishing

Mimi, Money and Me is written in a format that responds to many of the issues and concerns that some people face. It is highly recommended that you consult legal and financial advisors before implementing any recommendations or suggestions made in this book to determine whether they are right for you.

ISBN 978-0-9827037-0-0

Printed in the United States of America

To my dear Mother (Mimi),

with heartfelt thanks for

making us learn the rules of money,

despite our pleas not to have to.

ACKNOWLEDGMENTS

This book could not have come together without the help of a lot of people. I want to give each of them a sincere thank you for their help, encouragement, and support. Without them, *Mimi, Money and Me* never would have been completed.

First and foremost is my husband, Jim Davis. He has been my supporter and my rock since we met in high school, many years ago. Jim has observed my growth and development both as a person and as a finance professional. For many years, he has encouraged me to write this book. He reviewed it, made critical comments, provided sound advice and judgment, helped with the research, and, generally has been there when needed. For all of his support and guidance, I am eternally grateful.

My sisters, Beverly Tobias, Janet Briggs, and Denise (Nisey) Coleman, have each played a role in helping me get the book to this point. They have previewed the book, assisted in recalling the Mimi-isms, served as editors, and tried to help me better understand the human dimension of some of the situations I have faced with students and clients.

This book was enhanced by the contributions of three of my closest friends and colleagues--Kathleen Henschel and Lee Straus, both experienced finance professionals, and Annette Ferrell, a skilled banker. They each reviewed draft after draft with an eye toward accuracy, understandability, and readability. All three have been with me throughout this journey.

There are many other friends and colleagues to whom I would like to express my gratitude. You have had faith in me and have supported me on this road to making *Mimi, Money and Me* a completed work. I am grateful to all of you, from the bottom of my heart.

CONTENTS

TOPICAL INDEX

THE STORY BEHIND THE BOOK
(Mimi Said There'd be Days Like This)

My story started many years ago. I was born the fourth of five children into a two-parent home. We lost our father when I was just 14 years old. My siblings and I were fortunate (though we didn't think so at the time) to have been born to a smart woman (Mimi, as she came to be affectionately called) who understood the money game, knew how to play it, and was determined to teach her children its rules.

Even though he knew the rules, Daddy was far more lenient and much more generous with money than Mama was. He never was "the enforcer." At the time, we thought Mama was mean, stingy, and just didn't want to give us what we asked for. Little did we understand that: 1) she didn't have it to give us; 2) she was working diligently to stretch the money she did have; and 3) she was determined to teach us lessons to last a lifetime (and they have). She said, "The time will come when you will appreciate what I am trying to teach you." Boy, she was right!

Mimi had a saying for everything. I've listed many of her directives to us throughout the book where they seem to fit. I call them "Mimi-isms" and hope you will understand and appreciate them as much as we now do. Some of the sayings originated with her; others, perhaps not. But, all were a part of her way of teaching us valuable lessons about life and about how money works.

My earliest recollection of anything having to do with the subject of money goes back to when I was five years old. I saw what looked like a lot of change on my Mother's dresser and helped myself to a nickel, since I didn't think she would miss it. There were several things, though, that I didn't know: 1) she had just gotten change for a dollar; 2) she knew exactly how much she had on that dresser; and 3) she and I were the only two people in the house. When she noticed that five cents was missing, it pointed to only one person--me! I got the spanking of my life! (It was one of only two that I remember. The other was for coloring my lips on my first grade picture because I wanted to have on lipstick.) Boy, did I learn a lesson! Mother threatened to put me in reform school--a place for bad children back then--and I was scared to death.

That incident happened many years ago and I still remember it as though it were yesterday. There was no Judge Judy Sheindlin, Judge Joe Brown or Judge Greg Mathis to resolve money matters. We had our own judge, "Mimi Staunton." She was both our judge and jury. We learned that you did not touch things that did not belong to you; you returned anything you borrowed; and a whole host of other lessons including how to respect money. These lessons have been invaluable to each of us and we have passed them down to our children and to theirs.

Later in my life, I came to realize a lot of people, both old and young, were not so "lucky" as to have learned some of the money (and life) lessons Mimi taught us. Because I have seen the consequences of this, helping others learn these skills has become my passion--my life's work. I study it, talk about it, read about it, and write about it, incessantly.

Mimi, Money and Me is different than most of the money management books you've read. Written in plain English with an easy-to-follow format, its main purpose is to help you understand basic money matters which will equip you with the knowledge you need to make good financial decisions. In it, I teach you about money--the language of money, the rules of the money game and how to play it to win! I do not teach about investments, but leave that to the investment experts, since it is a discipline unto itself.

This book is the culmination of more than 30 years I've spent educating myself; conducting seminars from coast to coast; advising individuals and couples, both rich and poor; and listening to people talk about their hopes and fears as well as their misconceptions, mistakes and misunderstandings concerning money. I'm writing about things I've studied, things I know and care about, and things I personally practice.

Mimi, Money and Me is written in a format that responds to many of the issues and concerns I have heard over the years. However, I do suggest that you consult legal and financial advisors before implementing any of my recommendations or suggestions to determine whether they are right for you.

The book is divided into seven major topics, plus a "free for all." The areas covered are:

- Understanding Your Financial Value System (Knowing Yourself)

- Budgeting (Keeping Your Money Straight)

- Banking (Looking Out for the Nickels and Dimes)

- Credit (Using Other People's Money)

- Estate Planning (Planning for When the Will Matures)

- Real Estate (Keeping a Roof Over Your Head)

- Insurance (Protecting What You Have)

- Grab Bag (This and That)

You might be shocked at some of the things people don't know about money. Following are a few examples:

1. If you co-sign for anything for anybody, you are as liable for the repayment of the loan as the person who has the product or used the service. The vendor may come to you as soon as the first payment is missed, and odds are he will secure a judgment against you for the monies owed, plus interest and legal fees.

2. A written agreement cannot be changed with a verbal agreement. If you want to change the terms and conditions of a written agreement, the law says the change, too, must be done in writing.

3. If you add someone's name to your asset (such as your house or bank account) as a joint owner so there are two of you on the title or account, half of that asset legally belongs to the other person. You cannot remove that co-owner's name without their permission.

4. If you are several months behind on your car payment, the dealer probably will find the car, no matter how well you hide it. If not, the merchant can sue you in court and is very likely to win.

These are the kinds of tidbits you will find throughout the book. It is my sincere belief that many of you have never been taught these things; others may not care; but most of you just want knowledge.

For years, people who know me, my passion and my work have encouraged me to write this book. They tell me my empathetic way of listening to people describe their money issues, and my plain-English way of talking about money, make the subject easy to understand and much less intimidating. Plus, the "Mimi-isms" provide lots of food for thought and at least a few smiles.

There are many myths, misconceptions, mistakes, as well as misunderstandings involving money. This book is an accumulation of *101* of those I hear most often, along with the realities associated with each. It is a result of many years of experience and is presented in a way that I hope you find enjoyable, readable, understandable and enlightening.

I invite you to make ***Mimi, Money and Me*** a part of your GPS (global positioning system) as you travel along the road to financial independence. Remember, your financial freedom is up to you. Today's decisions become tomorrow's realities!

PREFACE

We live in a financially complex and demanding time. It is becoming increasingly difficult to live within one's income, these days, and to save for tomorrow. Nevertheless, it is essential we do just that in order to be healthy, both financially and emotionally.

Financial education is rarely a part of public school curricula, nor is it taught at home. Thus, many people are not equipped with the necessary knowledge and skills to successfully navigate life's financial waters.

Some people have little or no savings for either emergencies or retirement. Overextensions of credit are commonplace. Bankruptcies and foreclosures have skyrocketed. Most people have no budget or spending plan. Over half of the population with assets and/or dependents does not have a Will. With so many other demands on your financial resources, saving for college for yourself or your children is becoming increasingly difficult.

By pointing out some of the misinformation that exists and presenting realities associated with questions I've heard along the way, this book is designed to help equip you with the tools you will need for sound financial decision-making and independence. It speaks to money management principles that are essential to exist in today's complicated financial world. These principles include:

- Understand and create your own financial value system.
- Have written goals for yourself and identify your priorities.
- Develop and live by a budget or spending plan.
- Learn to live beneath your means.

17

- Develop sound credit and debt management practices and do not overspend. (Become self-reliant not credit-reliant.)

- Spend and invest wisely.

- Do not co-sign your good credit away.

- Save early; save often; and pay yourself first.

- Save for your own retirement.

As someone who has lived by these principles most of my life, I can assure you that if you step back, resolve to take control of your financial life, and practice the realities of the money game discussed in this book, you will indeed become financially successful. It's not that hard. Remember, achieving financial freedom is simply a matter of developing and practicing the right habits.

Happy reading!

Patricia

CHAPTER 1

UNDERSTANDING YOUR
FINANCIAL VALUE SYSTEM

UNDERSTANDING YOUR

FINANCIAL VALUE SYSTEM

Mimi-isms:

"A fool and his money are soon parted."[1]

"Every tub's got to stand on its own bottom."

"Learn to paddle your own canoe."

"It's better to have and not need than to need and not have"

"God bless the child that's got his own."[2]

---

[1] Thomas Tusser
[2] Billie Holiday and Arthur Herzog

> **#1. As a child, I grew up in a household where my parents were very tight-fisted with money. As a single adult, I spend freely with little concern about tomorrow. I believe I am likely to change and, one day, get back to my more conservative financial roots.**

REALITY

Perhaps you will; perhaps you won't. Understanding your financial value system--how you think about money, and why--is essential to managing your financial life well. The habits of many of the adults in our lives--mother, father, grandparents, spouses, ex-spouses, etc., along with our childhood experiences involving money, affect each of us, seriously impacting how we think about money. They form the basis of our family values. Sometimes, we become just like the adults who influenced us. Just as often, we become the exact opposite.

Are your behaviors those of a saver or a spender? Each can achieve financial success. Each has different triggers or stimuli. Most important to the saver is never running out of money. Most important to the spender is a desire to enjoy the pleasures of life, no matter what. Which of these do you identify with most?

To answer this question, first, you must resolve how you think about money--what having money means to you, what you want your money to do for you, and what your long-term life goals are. Only then will you be able to develop a system that gets both your financial goals and personal values in sync. This may mean reverting to those more conservative roots.   It is just as likely to mean developing a new paradigm that works for you--an adult who wants to take full control of and responsibility for your financial future.

By giving us an allowance, Mimi taught us how to budget. We didn't know that term while growing up, but we certainly know it now. A budget is the saver's "best friend." Fortunately, I married a guy who has the same attitudes about money that I have. To this day, we use a budget to direct our spending and to help us meet our goals.

When I think about Mimi's directive that we each had to learn to stand on our own two feet (to "paddle our own canoe"), I am reminded of another incident with her that has made me smile over the years. My husband and I were visiting for Christmas and were in her bedroom one afternoon, dressing to go out. Mimi knocked on the door and asked to come in, to put money in her piggy bank. I asked where she had gotten money since she had not been out of the house. She replied that her neighbor, Oscar, had given it to her. I asked why Oscar had given her money. She replied, "Because he used my phone." "You charge your neighbor to use your phone?" I asked, not believing what I had heard. "Yes, I do," she said, unapologetically. "Why?" I inquired. She said it was because there were three grown men in that house and they were too cheap to buy a phone.

"How much do you charge them?" I asked.   When she told me, I remarked that the amount was more than they would pay in a public phone booth. It was her witty reply to my last comment that makes me smile. She said, "I charge them more for several reasons: one, my house is warm in the winter and cool in the summer; two, I give them a comfortable place to sit down; three, I save them a two-block walk to the phone booth; four, they don't have to have exact change; and five, they don't have to use my phone if they don't want to!" Now, do you see why we thought she was mean? She was one savvy lady!

#2. I am engaged to a wonderful guy. Our biggest problem is we are opposites when it comes to how we think about money. He is carefree and spends almost everything he earns; I am more conservative and believe in putting something aside for a rainy day. Despite this difference, I think we can co-exist happily.

REALITY

When I do singles seminars, I always recommend that participants exchange FICO (credit) scores before exchanging wedding vows. A FICO score has a numerical value between 300 and 850 and was originally developed by Fair Isaac Corp. (founded by Bill Fair and Earl Isaac). It represents the evaluation of the information in your file at a credit bureau and judges your risk of default. The score helps lenders and others predict how likely you are to make your credit payments on time. The higher your credit score, the more likely you are to qualify for a loan; the lower the interest payment you will be charged by a lender; and the higher the credit limit will likely be that the lender will grant you. (See Appendix A for a description of the FICO credit scoring model--the one most widely used by lenders--and some tips for managing your credit score.)

There are three major credit bureaus that maintain credit information and to which creditors regularly report your spending and payment habits.

They are Equifax, Experian and TransUnion. You have three credit scores, one at each of the three credit bureaus. Though they may be slightly different because not all lenders report to each one, they tend to be in the same ballpark. The law says that once a year, any person can get one free credit report from each of the three bureaus. To do so, contact the credit bureau of choice or go on line to **www.annualcreditreport.com**. Be forewarned, the report is free, but you will have to pay to get the actual score. For your information, **www.freecreditreport.com** does not give you your credit report without charge, as their website name implies. (See Appendix B for contact information for the three credit bureaus.)

Let's get back to the original question. My suggestion that you exchange FICO scores may sound strange, but you need to know the spending habits of anyone with whom you are about to partner. It's one thing to have $100,000 in student loans. It's quite another to owe that same amount to Sears, Macy's, MasterCard, Wal-Mart or Brooks Brothers. And, if there ever has been something as serious as a bankruptcy, the other person certainly has a right to know before the wedding. (There's a lot to be done between the time you say, "I will" and the time you say, "I do!")

A credit score exchange serves as the basis for financial discussions that, hopefully, will force the two of you to talk about your attitudes about money; how you've handled your money in the past (and why); as well as how the two of you want your financial future together to work. Once you start having these kinds of open and honest discussions, you will develop an understanding of and appreciation for each other's point of view. This should pave the way for compromises that you both could find acceptable.

In his book, *Smart Couples Finish Rich,* author David Bach says, "According to the experts, the number one cause of divorce in this country is fighting over money." Working together on your financial goals not only increases the likelihood that the two of you will succeed financially, but it also improves your chances of living "happily ever after."

So, the answer is, yes, you two can co-exist happily if you do your homework. But, don't kid yourself. It might take several conversations; it might involve some pain; and neither of you is likely to get everything you want.

> *#3. If he loves me, we won't fight over money.*

REALITY

As Tina Turner's hit record asks, "What's Love Got to Do with It?" What is most important here is that you and your partner have open and honest discussions about your financial histories and your expectations for the future. You each should know how the other has (or has not) managed his or her personal finances and how, together, you can successfully manage them going forward. If your attitudes about money are very different from each other, this will require extra work to resolve. Not having these conversations early on can lead to unpleasant surprises later.

In the book referenced earlier, *Smart Couples Finish Rich,* author David Bach sums it up perfectly when he says, "...Without teamwork, financial planning for most couples becomes a battle, not a victory. And, ignoring the problem will only make it worse." As one of my colleagues, Maria, said to her new husband when he seemed uninterested in the whole concept of financial management, "… Budgeting is not a spectator sport. Either get off the bleachers and into the game, or go home!"

In another case I know of, it was not until the couple went to close on their home that the new wife discovered her spouse's earlier bankruptcy, that he had been married before, and that he was under a child support order. All of these things had a serious impact on his credit record and now, perhaps, on hers. Imagine the arguments that occurred that evening and beyond! (I suspect the problem, here, was much greater than just financial omissions.)

> *#4. My friend and I are about to move in together. One of us thinks we should have written agreements; the other says no. Who's right?*

REALITY

These days, living together outside of marriage is as common an occurrence as a married couple was in our parents' and grandparents' days. Unmarried, co-habiting couples may be young, old, heterosexual, same sex, just friends or any combination of the above. In most circles, yesterday's stigma of living together outside of marriage no longer exists. That having been said, your question seems to center around whether there are protections each of you needs as you enter into this living arrangement. Indeed, there are.

Understanding Your Financial Value System

Let's assume that you and your friend will buy property together, perhaps have joint bank accounts, obtain credit and accumulate other things of value. You need to have written agreements detailing who owes and who owns what as well as how things will be divided should the relationship not work out. Unlike married couples, you may not have any automatic legal protections (unless you are in a common-law state). Therefore, without written agreements as described above, you might not have the protection you may need.

Imagine, for a moment, that you pooled your resources to buy a home but your friend is the only one listed on the title. What do you suppose will happen if you decide to go your separate ways? Legally, the house belongs to the one who is listed on the title and the other has no recourse. Even if you can prove that you helped make the monthly payments, the property still belongs to the titleholder and you have no legal claim to any of the equity in the house. This is the reason you both need to make certain that "what if" possibilities are thought through, in advance, and written agreements are prepared and signed. That way, neither of you will end up feeling taken advantage of.

> *#5. My fiancé thinks we should have joint credit cards and I say no. He says there is no risk in merging our credit since we intend to marry one day.*

REALITY

Many people think the way your fiancé does. But, you both should be aware that this poses several risks. First, the relationship may not work out and you may have to untangle a mess. Second, if you get joint cards, legally, you each will be responsible for the entire debt, regardless of who actually made the purchases. Third, your spending habits may be very different. You each should establish your own credit history in your own name. After your wedding is soon enough to open joint accounts.

Here's a case in point. Jacob and Janet dated for several years during college and decided to marry. In anticipation of the wedding, they jointly applied for credit and purchased things for the new apartment using their new credit cards. Fast-forward six months. You guessed it. One of them found someone else. It was then that the arguments began over who had paid for what; who would pay for what; and who would keep what. Had they used separate credit cards and determined who would have responsibility for certain items, at least that part of the break-up would have been easier.

Many years ago when my spouse and I became engaged, he took responsibility for purchasing the bedroom set and I agreed to buy the dining room set. (There was no money for living room furniture. But, we knew that with these two purchases, at least we would have someplace to eat and someplace to sleep.) We put our respective purchases in layaway with an agreement to have our items paid for by the time of the wedding. And, we did!

> *#6. I don't believe in saving. Because credit cards are always available and I can pay for things over time, there is no reason for me to save.*

REALITY

Putting money away for a rainy day is just plain smart and is something everybody should do, for several reasons. A few are:

1. Saving is good discipline for life and is the best way to get ahead. Setting savings goals is no different than setting life goals. You set a target and map out a strategy to get you there within a defined time period. You know exactly where you will be on the target date, if you follow the plan.

2. Saving is a great way to take care of your personal finances. It is the vehicle for putting money aside for the things you want and helps ensure the money will be available if and when you need it.

3. Having an emergency fund (representing six months or more of living expenses) means you will have money to get you through drastic situations like a job loss, major illness or the death of the primary breadwinner.

First, you must make the decision to save. Then, you have to figure out how much money to save, where it will come from, and where to put it so it is safe and will earn money for you.

There is good news regarding the savings habits of U.S. citizens. According to a recent *Wall Street Journal* report, by the first quarter of 2009, U.S. families finally had started to save again. The U.S. savings rate for most of 2009 was in the 3 to 5 percent range. (It had been on the decline since the mid-1980s. For much of the time since then, it actually was below zero.)

However, in comparison to other countries, the U.S. savings rate, though getting better, is still notoriously low. National savings rates in Europe are believed to average around 20 percent while Japan's rate averages close to 25 percent. The International Monetary Fund estimates that China has a national savings rate of almost 50 percent.

In our country, credit cards are generally available as long as your credit remains good. However, a credit crisis makes future credit much harder to get, especially at good rates. There even may come a time when you no longer can get credit or when your existing cards are maxed out. If that happens, you need to have a ready source of funds to make necessary purchases so you can take care of yourself. Counting on financing your lifestyle (buying now and paying later) is a dangerous outlook to have and does not lead to good financial health.

> #7. *I have a decent job and not many expenses. I should be able to spend $5 to $10 a day on lunch if I want to.*

REALITY:

Buying lunch every day is costly, especially given the alternative of bringing lunch from home most days and then splurging, say, once a week. Let's do the math. Assume there are 46 work weeks in the year after allowing for 6 weeks of vacation, sick days, and holidays. This equals 230 workdays (46 weeks x 5 days). At your average cost of $7.50 (halfway between $5 and $10), you spend slightly more than $1,700 a year on daily lunch purchases. If you were to carry your lunch from home and save even $1,500 of this amount, your bank account would be richer by a nice tidy sum.

> **#8.** *I think it's time to start teaching my seven-and nine-year-olds about money. Others think they are too young. Are they?*

REALITY

I don't think it's ever too early to begin teaching children about money. As I mentioned earlier, when we were very young, Mimi insisted my siblings and I learn about how money works and develop a healthy respect for money. The allowance system she used formed the basics of money management for all of us. We are now so very grateful for all she taught us.

Our Mother's payday every two weeks was our "allowance day." I don't remember her ever not giving us our allowance. But, if we ran out of money before the two weeks were up, too bad. I can vividly recall a lecture from my younger days when I pleaded with her for extra money because I had spent all I had before the two weeks were up. The conversation went very matter-of-factly like this:

"Patricia, I work for the Department of Labor. I get paid every other Monday. If I run out of money before payday,

31

the Department of Labor gives me no more money. They don't care. Now, the same thing applies to you. You get your allowance every other Monday. You know when you get it how long it will be before you get some more. If you choose to spend all of your money before payday, shame on you. But, you get no more money. I don't care!"

Recently, one of my sisters and I were talking about our Mother and how strict she was with us about money. I remarked that even though she wouldn't give us additional money, she might consider making us a loan. My sister recalled, "Yes, but, first, you had to get the lecture." If your allowance was a dollar and you needed a dime, the lecture went something like this: "If you can't live off of a dollar for two weeks, how will you live off of ninety cents? This is a loan; it is not a gift. And, you're going to pay me my dime back!" Next allowance day, she didn't give you a dollar and hope you remembered you owed her a dime. She remembered and gave you ninety cents!

I told you she was one tough lady! That's why we had to learn to budget our money. It didn't matter how much the allowance was. Basically, we had to make what we had last or else do without.

So, you see, teaching kids about money involves more than just counting coins. It involves teaching them about saving, spending, giving, investing and respecting money. Developing discipline is a very important part of this teaching.

I am licensed to teach a financial literacy program called "Camp Millionaire." It is a one- to five-day program, filled with fun and games, and teaches kids, teens and adults about money. In that program, using age-appropriate language, we teach such things as:

Understanding Your Financial Value System

- The many roles of money

- The rules of the game of money

- How to live within your means (allowances and budgets)

- How to use your money to create the life you want

- Money beliefs--what some of them are and where they come from

- Types of income--earned versus passive

- The three pillars of wealth--real estate, business and the stock market

- Needs versus wants

- Using other people's money--credit

- Making dream boards—envisioning what you want your tomorrow to look like

To date, under the Creative Wealth International banner, Camp Millionaire has taught thousands of people--ages 8 to 80--the rules of the money game. The organization is committed to providing financial education to people worldwide, but, children, teens and women are a major program focus. You can go online to **www.creativewealthintl.org** to learn about program offerings in your area as well as other financial education products they offer.

Another valuable resource for financial literacy tools for young people is the website for an organization called NEFE--the National Endowment for Financial Education--at **www.nefe.org**. NEFE is a "...private, non-profit, national foundation wholly dedicated to improving the financial well-being of all Americans" and provides lots of useful, free information.

Another company that offers financial education programs for young adults is the Society for Financial Education and Professional Development (SFEPD)--at **www.sfepd.org**. One of its key programs is directed at college students, nationwide. Each year, SFEPD reaches thousands of students to ensure they have the financial knowledge and skills needed to maximize their education. The U.S Treasury Department, Office of Financial Education, has presented SFEPD with a Certificate of Recognition for its work. The founder and President of SFEPD sits on the President's Advisory Council on Financial Literacy.

This type of instruction, Camp Millionaire, NEFE, SFEPD or some other program, helps give people of all ages a basis for developing the solid money sense that is critical to have going forward. However, where kids are concerned, the best thing you can do for them is to lead by example. As they get older and can absorb more, teach them more. Early on, make discussions about money a family affair and give your youngster a head start on his or her journey toward financial freedom. You both will be glad you did.

CHAPTER 2

BUDGETING

BUDGETING

Mimi-isms:

"Money spent is money gone."

"You can't spend it but once."

"Save some for a rainy day."

> **#9. People who follow a budget are no more likely to meet their financial goals than are those who do not.**

REALITY

My experience is that just the opposite is true. People who follow a budget not only are more likely to meet their financial goals, but also they spend less, save more, pay with cash or pay off their credit cards at the end of each billing cycle.

Budgeters are comfortable setting priorities, making choices and, in general, are willing to accept responsibility for themselves and their families. They seem to understand and live by the old adage that says, "When your outgo exceeds your income, your upkeep will be your downfall!"

> **#10. Having a budget is too restrictive. That's why many people hate them.**

REALITY

First, let's talk about what a budget is and what it is not. A budget is not a straight-jacket or a shackle. It is not an inflexible tool. Most of all, it is not a plan that must be followed forever, no matter what.

A budget is a step-by-step plan for meeting your expenses during a given period of time. If done properly, it covers a 6- to 12-month timeframe and provides an at-a-glance summary of all of your income and expenses during that period. It reveals where you may have the flexibility to alter your spending.

It also helps you account for money that just seems to trickle away. It provides a way for family members to talk about financial goals for the household and the role of each in achieving them. Plus, it provides you with a roadmap for gaining control over your money. A budget is flexible and should be adjusted as your life changes.

Once all your known and anticipated income/expenses for the selected period are listed, a budget can help reduce stress due to money worries. If you follow the roadmap you create, then your financial life can operate, essentially, on auto-pilot. (See Appendix C for a sample budget format with instructions on how to create one.)

I will admit to being a master budgeter. As a finance professional, I have done hundreds of budgets in corporate America, for clients in my financial advisory practice and for my family.

Allow me to use my household of two adults as an example. Usually, around November, my husband and I start discussing financial goals for the next year--places we want to go, things we want to do and out-of-the-ordinary expenses we might incur. This conversation continues off and on over the next few weeks. By early December, our decisions have been converted into dollars and a draft of the next year's budget is done. Then, we let it rest until the new year's tax rates, other deductions and the prior year-end expenses are known. By the end of January, the budget is set for the year, pending major life changes.

Because we have been doing this for a long time and know our spending patterns, few surprises come up during the year. There are times when we may decide to do something that is unplanned. But, because we are savers, spontaneous decisions usually can be funded from savings. I can proudly say that we never, ever overspend. If we don't have the money, we don't spend it.

As I tell my clients, "When you can do better, you do better-- not the other way around." That means you don't spend first and hope your income is sufficient to cover your expenditures. With a budget, you are certain to match the two at the outset.

> **#11. Budgets are an individual effort, not a family affair.**

REALITY

The idea that creating a family budget is a solo activity is a misconception and a mistake unless you are single. When families construct a budget together and everyone is intimately aware of its contents, then they are all on the same page. Regardless of how much is earned, there needs to be a structured way of keeping track of income and expenses, and of making all family members aware of what can and cannot be done financially.

One November, a client who was a 40-year old divorced mother of a 9-year old son, wanted to do a 12-month budget for the next year. After including all the income and expenses she expected, she was several thousands of dollars short. Of course, there are only two solutions: 1) generate more income; or 2) cut expenses. Reluctantly, she chose the latter. She had no idea where the cuts could be made. That's where I came in.

First, I suggested the housekeeper had to go (or agree to work for free). She unhappily agreed. Second to go were 9-year old Zack's $100+ sneakers. However, getting rid of those two expenses still wasn't enough to bring her outgo in line with her income.

Third to go were Zack's daily trips to McDonald's. Grandpa picked Zack up every day from school, but Zack didn't like to eat what grandpa had in the house. So, Zack's mother spent lots of money on after-school trips to McDonald's for both Zack and grandpa. I recommended that she stock grandpa's cupboard with whatever she and Zack wanted him to eat, and cut out the daily trips for fast food. (Plus, eating in fast-food restaurants so often not only was a budget-killer for her, but also, it was unhealthy for both Zack and grandpa.)

Finally, Zack was given a choice--piano lessons, basketball camp or summer camp. He couldn't have them all. Sitting her son down and explaining to him about her finances helped Zack understand more about financial matters and gave him a role to play in keeping their expenses more in line with what they could afford.

Having these kinds of discussions ultimately made it easier on my client, since her son then understood more about the money game and its realities, and had a role in making the process work. Along the way, Zack learned some valuable money management lessons. (And, so did his mom.)

After having made these changes to the budget, income and expenses were in balance.

> **#12. The only people who need budgets are those who can't make ends meet.**

REALITY

I believe every individual who has access to money needs to have a budget. A well-constructed budget that reflects your financial reality provides the information needed to gain control over your money. It clearly shows when and where your money is coming from, as well as when and where your money is going. It helps you use unexpected money wisely and promotes family togetherness.

John and Becky are a high-powered, relatively young, professional couple with two small children. Becky, a lawyer, earns about $250,000 a year; John, a product salesman, earns close to $125,000 annually. Despite their high salaries, they saved virtually none of their income. Becky's attitude is that she works hard and should have everything she wants--and boy, does she want stuff! John thought they should have a budget and was concerned that they didn't have anything saved for a rainy day. This prompted him to contact me.

When we sat down to develop their budget, imagine my shock (even to this day) when they told me that they spend $400 a month on dry cleaning and laundry! It turned out that Becky did not change out of her work clothes when she came home, and she played with the two tots in her business clothes. A simple question from me was a shocker to her. "Why don't you change your clothes?" She had never thought about it.

You can see it is not just people who have limited resources who need to evaluate how they are spending/not spending and saving/not saving their money. It doesn't make sense for a family with two small children to have an income level that puts them in the top one percent of wage earners in this country, to have nothing put aside for a rainy day or for their family's future. As I told them, their current earnings level is not promised forever.

So, save for emergencies; save for tomorrow; and be prepared to take care of yourself should darker days lie ahead.

#13. Making a budget is easy. All you have to do is guess what your income and expenses will be during the time period covered by the budget.

REALITY

Make no mistake; putting together a budget is hard work. It is not a guessing game. To do it properly, you need to gather a lot of information about past expenses and spending habits, and develop goals for the period covered by the budget. You need to look back at 6 to12 months of expenses to determine both the categories and amounts of income and expenses to be reflected in your budget. You use items like:

- Check registers
- Bank and credit card statements

- Bill stubs, such as utilities, rent, mortgage, insurance, child care, repairs, property taxes, gasoline, personal items, gifts, insurance, medical expenses, and transportation (including car payments, if any, repair/maintenance charges, tags, etc.)
- Tax returns
- Pay stubs
- Your written goals for the next 6 to 12 months and the costs associated with each

Use all of these pieces of information to put together the first draft of a budget that realistically reflects your (or your family's) income and expenditure patterns. Remember the saying, "GIGO" which means "Garbage In, Garbage Out." The budget won't be helpful to you if it isn't real. (See Appendix C for specific budgeting instructions and a sample format you can tailor fit to your situation.) Then make the adjustments needed to bring it into balance.

> **#14. When I retire, I expect my expenses to drop significantly. So, I will be able to live on much less than I do today.**

REALITY

"How much will I need in retirement?" is probably the question I get asked most often in my pre-retirement seminars. Newsflash! A survey by the *Wall Street Journal* showed that while some individuals live comfortably on 75 percent of their pre-retirement income, many retirees

(75 percent) said their financial needs equal or exceed their spending during their working years. Almost half had expected their expenses to be lower.

I tell seminar participants to expect that the "dollar amount of your spending will not change in retirement, but the character of your spending will." What does that mean? It means that while you may not have work-related expenses such as commute costs, daily lunch expenses and/or dry cleaning costs, you will have several other expenses that will be higher than before, and some you did not have at all. For example, after retirement, you may want to do several things you did not have time to do while working, such as extensive travel, more frequent short trips to see the kids and grandkids, and golf or dance lessons.

In addition, you may have higher healthcare costs for both premiums and co-pays, higher utility costs due to higher usage (since you're home more often), and greater regular food costs due to eating more meals at home. In addition, though the house may now be paid for, you have a 25- to 30-year-old house with higher maintenance expenses, such as a new roof or appliances. The same can be said for your paid-for, but aging automobile. There probably will be higher maintenance costs due to its age and the expiration of the manufacturer's warranty.

As you can see, the analysis can be a little tricky. There is no "one size fits all." You need to think about how you want to live in retirement and prepare a written, post-retirement budget with all the elements of income and expense in it that are needed to accurately reflect your anticipated post-retirement financial life. Only then can you see in black and white how much money you will need in order to pay for your retirement lifestyle.

Budgeting

Appendix D provides a sample calculation of retirement funding needs. There are several critical factors in the calculation:

1. How much longer do you expect to work to be able to save additional retirement resources?

2. What do you expect your annual expenditure level to be in retirement?

3. What do you anticipate your income level to be, including pension, Social Security and other retirement income?

4. What is the current value of your investment assets?

5. What is the current value of your retirement assets?

6. What growth rate do you want to use on your current and post retirement investments?

7. What inflation rate do you want to assume?

Once all of these variables are factored in, you should be able to determine your bi-weekly/monthly/annual savings needs to fund the retirement lifestyle you want. If this amount is too much of a stretch for you, then you might have to either scale back the level of expenditures or decide to postpone your retirement date by a few years.

There are numerous online retirement funding calculators. Bloomberg, Fidelity, AARP and MSN Money are a few that are easily accessible and simple to use. When all is said and done, they provide you with the answers you seek regarding how much you need to have for retirement based upon your financial choices and parameters.

Mimi, Money and Me

CHAPTER 3

BANKING

BANKING

#15. Banks do not make mistakes; so, there really is no need for me to look closely at my bank statement.

REALITY

This is false and is a common misconception--one that could cost you dearly. By closely examining your monthly statement, not only might you discover a mistake or two, but also you will become aware of the size and frequency of bank charges you are incurring.

Most check processing done by U.S. banks is done manually, not with optical scanners. A human being sits at an encoding machine and types/encodes the check or deposit amount at the bottom of your processed checks and deposit slips. This is the information read by machines later in the process, not your handwriting.

Industry-wide, the error rate in check processing operations centers is about one percent. This means if your bank processes 10 million checks per month, its processors make, on average, close to 100,000 errors per month. While most banks have Error Corrections Units whose job it is to fix processor errors, a few mistakes may be made that the encoder and the Error Corrections Unit accidentally miss. If the encoder makes an undetected error, the error becomes a part of the information carried forward throughout the rest of the processing of the check or deposit. So, your account could be hit with an incorrect amount.

If you never look at your bank statement, you might not pick this up and your checkbook could reflect a balance that is out of sync with the bank's. Regular checkbook balancing is a way of ensuring that you and the bank are both working with the same information. If not, then you have what you need to start an inquiry to determine the cause of the discrepancy.

The same is true when it comes to fees. Many people overlook ATM, overdraft and non-sufficient funds (NSF) fees. By closely examining your bank statement, you can easily view these fees, enter them into your checkbook, and be certain your calculations are based on the correct figures. You also may uncover fees charged to your account that are incorrect.

I had one client who had $242 in bank fees on his checking account statement in one month. He forgot his overdraft protection cost him $39 each time he activated it. Although he had no money in his account at the time, twice a month, he typically made a $20 withdrawal for each of the 3 days immediately preceding his bi-weekly payday, for a total of $117 in fees to withdraw $60! If he had withdrawn all $60 at once, at least he would have incurred only one $39 fee. He had no idea his actions were costing him that much money until I unsealed and reviewed his account statement with him. Of course, he could avoid the overdraft fees altogether if he didn't have the overdraft protection. But that would mean more serious money management to ensure he had sufficient funds when he needed them, and that he did not spend money he didn't have. Imagine that!

Another client lives in Maryland; works in Washington, D.C.; and has her paycheck direct deposited into a bank in Pennsylvania, thereby generating a large number of "foreign" ATM charges. When I asked why she uses an out-of-state bank, she replied that her grandparents had started the Pennsylvania bank many years ago and she felt an emotional attachment to it. I suggested she emotionally attach herself to that bank with a savings account and find a local bank where her paycheck could be deposited. With her current arrangement, she always had to incur a charge to get her own funds. What a huge waste of money!

> **#16. ATM fees are costing me a fortune. I can't do anything to lower them.**

REALITY

You don't have to incur ATM fees. Though it takes discipline, you can write yourself a check once a week to cover your budgeted/anticipated cash needs. That way you will have the cash to pay for your expenses and not need an ATM. But, remember you have to make this amount last for the entire week. **(Mimi would tell you, "You know how long that money has to last. If you run out, shame on you!")**

If taking out cash on a weekly basis doesn't work for you, there still are ways to minimize your ATM fees. Look on the back of your ATM card for the logo that indicates which ATM network your bank belongs to. While you may be charged by the in-network bank, at least your bank will not charge you an out-of-network fee. A better alternative would be to choose a local bank or credit union that belongs to a network that allows free use of ATMs in the network.

There are surcharge-free networks like Star, Allpoint and Co-op Financial that claim to have thousands of ATMs nationwide. Another alternative is to use banks such as Metropolitan Bank and Schwab Bank that are not a part of any network but will reimburse you for ATM charges you incur.

There is one other way to avoid ATM fees. Use only your bank's ATMs. Usually, there is no charge for their use unless you use them excessively or have an account that restricts your usage. One final thought—go inside the bank for the cash needed. No ATM fees.

> **#17. It takes, on average, three days for a local check to clear. Therefore, I do not have to have the funds in my account for at least a couple of days after I write a check.**

REALITY

It no longer takes local checks up to three days to clear. Under the Check Clearing for the 21st Century Act that went into effect in October 2004, your checks could clear your bank within hours instead of days. Thus, the float you may once have had no longer exists.

Under the 2004 law, banks can make digital copies of your checks and transmit the information through the checking system. They, then, can destroy the actual check. In some cases, a merchant merely digitizes your check and gives it right back to you before you leave the store.

However, under this law, banks are not required to credit your account with deposits any more quickly than they did before the law. Thus, they are permitted to speed up withdrawals without speeding up the processing of deposits. Consumers Union estimates that this law results in millions of bounced checks and millions of dollars in associated bank fees.

There are several ways you can protect yourself:

1. Understand your bank's check and deposit processing schedule.

2. Don't write checks unless you are certain you have the money in your account at the time you write them.

3. Balance your checkbook every month to ensure there is no "double processing" of the checks you have written, since the bank may accidentally process both the electronic version of your check and the original paper copy.

4. Understand that out-of-town or very large checks you deposit still might take several days to be credited to your account.

If your bank makes a mistake, the law says they must make the correction to your account within 10 business days of your notification along with proof of the error, and that you must notify them of the error within 60 days. For specific instructions, you should read the Terms and Conditions found as a part of your electronic and/or paper statement in the area generally termed "In Case of Error."

#18. Debit cards are always better to use than credit cards because I don't have to pay interest on my purchases.

REALITY

Debit cards are not always better to use than credit cards. There may be benefits to both. Credit cards allow you to buy now and pay later (without interest charges, if you pay the bill in full each month). You are actually borrowing money from the card issuer who has paid the merchant, on your behalf, and you pay the money back to them. One of the major benefits is that they offer very generous protections against fraudulent charges. (Credit card laws and practices are discussed, in detail, in the next chapter.)

On the other hand, debit cards look like credit cards but operate very differently. Using a debit card is the same as paying cash. Funds are withdrawn from your bank account immediately, at the time of purchase, for the total amount. There never are interest charges attached. With a debit card, you don't have to carry cash or checks and the card provides instant access to your money worldwide.

However, there are a few debit card pitfalls which you should be aware of:

1. If you spend more than you have in your account, you may be allowed to make the purchase, but also you may incur substantial non-sufficient funds (NSF) fees. According to a recent *Consumer's Union* report, "...a person using a debit card more than 20 times per year pays an average of $223 in bounced check/overdraft fees. The one who doesn't use a debit card at all pays an average of $40."

2. Debit card features--instant access to your money and, often, no required PIN (personal identification number)--make fraud much easier (and potentially more costly) than is the case with a credit card. Your bank account can be quickly drained if your debit card is lost or stolen and you do not report the loss to your bank immediately. However, the law limits your liability for unauthorized use of your debit card to $50 if reported within 2 days after you discover it missing. It increases that amount to $500 if you report it after 2 days but less than 60 days. Your

liability becomes your entire account balance if you fail to report an unauthorized transfer within 60 days after your bank statement containing the unauthorized use is mailed to you. (Your maximum liability under federal law for the unauthorized use of a credit card, on the other hand, is $50.)

3. Unlike what happens with the use of a credit card, if you have a problem with the purchased merchandise or service, there is no credit card company available to help you to resolve an issue with the vendor. For example, if the merchandise is defective, is not as represented, or you want to return it according to the return policy but the vendor won't allow you to, you may have to work that out by yourself.

    A credit card issuer often will give you a temporary credit in the event of a dispute, and will hold up payment to the vendor until the matter has been resolved to your satisfaction. When you use a debit card to buy something, this option does not exist. That is, the bank usually does not temporarily refund your cash.

So, you can see, there are pluses and minuses to using debit cards. You have to decide which is better, debit or credit, given your particular situation.

#19. My bank automatically signed me up for overdraft protection and says I have no choice but to keep it.

REALITY

That is not correct. In November, 2009, the Federal Reserve passed a law effective July 1, 2010, that bans banks from charging overdraft fees unless customers sign up for the service. This decision was in response to many complaints from consumers about excessive overdraft fees they were being charged, often for very small overages, and even though they had not signed up for overdraft protection. After the law takes effect, banks must send consumers a notice explaining their overdraft policies and fees. You then must be given the option of signing up for the service if you want it. It no longer can be automatic.

Overdraft fees have become a multibillion-dollar revenue stream for financial institutions. The Center for Responsible Lending estimates that banks and credit unions collected nearly $24 billion in 2008 from overdraft protection charges. By the Center's calculations, that's more than $1 in fees for every $1 lent to consumers. Some consumers may welcome the service, even when it has not been requested. But others don't, especially if they find themselves paying hundreds of dollars in charges for a series of small transactions. (Overdraft fees are costly. They average close to $35 per occurrence.)

It is true that overdraft fees are a convenient way to guard against the embarrassment and costs associated with returned checks. But, careful account management is the least expensive way of protecting your money and of avoiding those fees.

CHAPTER 4

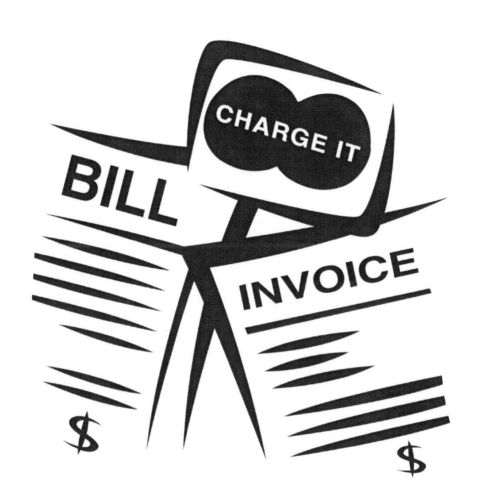

CREDIT

CREDIT

Mimi-isms:

"A loan is a loan; it is not a gift."

"Neither a borrower nor a lender be."[3]

"If you need to borrow it, you need to have your own of it."

---

[3] William Shakespeare's Hamlet, Act1, Scene 3

#20. Being able to get credit is an entitlement I have just by virtue of being an adult who has or has had a job.

REALITY

This statement, though felt by many, is definitely not true. Credit is a privilege that is offered to you based on your commitment that you can pay back what you borrow and are willing to do so. Being a working adult is only one piece of the puzzle. Credit allows you to borrow *tomorrow's* money to pay for something you get *today*. Credit also is a *promise* to repay a debt, usually with interest. Creditors want and expect to be paid back on time, and have every right to do so.

In one of my classes, an unemployed participant had extensive overdue credit but wasn't the least bit concerned about being delinquent or about when she would repay her debts. Her attitude was, "They have to understand; I don't have a job. So, they just have to wait!"

No, "they" (your creditors) don't "have to understand." It is you who has to understand. First, you have a responsibility to pay them. By extending you credit, they have lived up to their end of the agreement; now, they expect you to live up to yours. Second, when you can't, it is your duty to contact them to set up a payment schedule that you can (and will) keep. Third, if you do not repay your creditors and it becomes clear to them you have no intention of doing so, expect to have your items repossessed or for you to be taken to court so they can secure a garnishment or lien. Also, it is unlikely that you will be allowed further credit by them or others until you resolve your issues, regardless of your employment situation.

I recall one situation in which a couple depleted her pre-tax retirement account (401(k)) and used the money for a new home already under contract; then she lost her job. Instead of biting the bullet, taking the loss, and canceling the contract for the new home, they used ALL the cash withdrawn to furnish the new house. They did not put aside money for either taxes on the 401(k) withdrawal or for the 10 percent early withdrawal penalty assessed since she was younger than 59½ and this was not their first house. (See Reality #101 for a discussion of pre-tax retirement accounts and laws related to withdrawals from them.)

You can figure out the rest of the story. When the taxes on the early withdrawal were assessed, they could not pay them. The couple made an agreement with the IRS to pay $500 per month and did not live up to their part of the deal. Needless to say, this created a worse problem for them. After several delinquency notices went unanswered, Uncle Sam sent a notice that their house was going on the auction block if they did not pay the entire balance within 30 days! When I asked why they did not keep up the monthly IRS payment, as agreed, the reply was that they could not afford $500 a month. When I inquired as to why they had agreed to such a hefty payment, the response was, "We had to tell them something!"

That is no way to deal with creditors, especially the IRS. When you make an agreement, the expectation is that you are committing to keep it. Otherwise, expect the consequences to turn out badly for you, including losing the asset you were so desperately trying to protect.

---

21. Credit card over-the-limit fees are assessed only if my balance exceeds the limit at the end of the billing cycle.

REALITY

According to a recent Government Accountability Office study, about two-thirds of the major card issuers studied charge fees if your balance exceeds the credit limit *at any time* during the billing cycle. The rest of them charge a fee only if your balance exceeds the limit at the *end* of the billing cycle.

Also, the limit may be different depending upon the type of credit extended. For example, purchases, cash advances and transfers from another account all may have different limits. Be sure you read the fine print in your credit card agreement so you know exactly what the Terms and Conditions stipulate with each card you have. They may differ from card to card.

#22. I have a lot of credit cards I don't use. A friend suggested that I close those accounts. I think I should keep them open just in case I need them one day. Which one of us is correct?

REALITY

You are both partly correct. Having a large number of open credit cards can look bad on your credit report and can actually lower your credit score. That's because with so many open accounts, creditors know that, at any moment, you can run up each of them to their maximum credit limit.

But, don't close all of the accounts you are not using at one time. Gradually, close some of them, starting with the newest one. Why? Because the length of your credit history is a key component in calculating your credit score. (See Appendix A for a description of the FICO credit scoring model.)

Also, credit agencies look at something called your "credit utilization ratio," which is the percentage of the total amount of credit available to you that you are actually using. If you suddenly start closing accounts but do not pay down any of the remaining ones, that percentage will go up. Though we do not know for sure (because Fair Isaac Corp., the folks who developed the credit scoring model most widely used, won't reveal all their secrets), the word on the street is that your ratio of used credit to available credit should be in the 30 percent or lower range because that shows you are using much less than half the credit available to you. So, be sure to take that ratio into consideration as you start closing accounts.

#23. If I get a credit card solicitation that says I have been "pre-approved," that means I definitely will get the card.

REALITY:

When you are "pre-approved" for a credit card, it only means you have passed the first level of screening. It will not be until the credit card company looks at your credit report that it will decide the amount of credit, if any, it will extend to you. It may be a modest amount of $1,000 (or less) or a much larger amount of $10,000 (or more), depending upon what they find. If you read the fine print, usually, there is a provision that allows the credit card company to deny you any credit at all, depending upon whether you meet their approval criteria for the card.

#24. There is no advantage to having a gold, platinum, or black credit card.

REALITY

These cards are different than the standard American Express, MasterCard or Visa cards. Whether or not you call it an advantage to have them depends upon your perspective. First, they usually carry a higher annual fee than the same company's standard card. Second, the limits on these cards often far exceed the limits on standard cards. Third, some of these cards carry added benefits such as rewards, rebates and frequent flyer miles. Finally, the card issuer may provide you with an itemized, categorized listing of your expenses at year-end, which can be helpful to the business traveler in preparing personal tax returns or when making a budget.

#25. A "grace period" gives me a full 30 days from the date of purchase to pay the credit card bill before interest charges are applied to my account.

REALITY

Let's first define the term "grace period." A "grace period" is the time between the last date of your billing cycle and the due date of your payment. If the credit card company has not received the balance in full by the due date, then you will be charged interest. If you pay the full amount of the bill by the due date, then, usually, you are not charged interest for that billing cycle unless there have been cash advances during the period. Interest on cash advances is normally calculated from the date of the each advance to the date repayment is received.

You must read your contract carefully and pay strict attention to the due date shown on your monthly bill to ensure you pay in a timely manner. Your credit rating depends on it. (See Reality #26 for an update on the Credit Card Accountability Responsibility and Disclosure Act of 2009 that impacts this.)

#26. The Credit Card Act of 2009 is just more of the same old rules restated and will not make any difference to me as a consumer.

REALITY

The "Credit Card Accountability Responsibility and Disclosure Act of 2009" (CARD) that took effect in February 2010 was approved by Congress in July 2009 and contains some serious and much-needed reforms. CARD is designed to provide consumers protection against some of the lesser-known practices of credit card companies as well as some which have been determined to be grossly unfair and punitive.

The first set of CARD protections kicked in on August 20, 2009. In summary, these were:

1. Card issuers must provide 45 days notice of changes in the "Terms and Conditions" of your contract before they can take effect.

2. Credit card statements must be sent out at least 21 days before they are due (up from 14 days).

3. If there are changes in the terms of your contract, you have the right to pay off balances under the old terms of your agreement.

While each of us still has the duty to exhibit sound financial management practices and habits, and to exercise good judgment and personal responsibility, CARD's added clarity and extra protections are helpful to the consumer. Following is a more detailed account of some of CARD's provisions:

1. Credit card companies must give cardholders more time to pay their monthly bills. Payments cannot be due sooner than 21 days after the customer's statement is mailed. This means the "grace period" is lengthened and starts with the mailing date of your billing statement rather than the end of the billing cycle.

2. When you get a promotional rate for a portion of your balance, the introductory rate must be applied to the debt with the highest interest rate. For those who carry a balance with different rates (such as for cash advances versus regular purchases), this means it will be possible to pay off the overall balance a bit faster because the debt with the highest rate is getting the promotional rate, and you will pay less in total interest charges.

3. Historically, credit card companies have employed something called "universal default," which is the practice of raising interest rates on your credit card based on your payment record with unrelated creditors such as utility companies, mortgage companies and other credit card issuers. Being late on even one other payment could trigger interest rate hikes on all your credit cards. This did not change with the implementation of CARD.

   What changed is the way the interest rate hike is applied. The new rules say that unless you are 60 days delinquent on your credit card account, the new interest rate only can be applied to new charges. Interest on your old balance has to remain at your old rate. As long as you stay current, the new interest rate will not apply to your old balances.

4. Before CARD, credit card companies could change interest rates, rewards programs and other terms of the credit card agreement at any time, for no reason, without notice. CARD requires that they give you 45 days notice before they can make such changes. This may allow you sufficient time to pay off balances before the new rate/terms become effective.

5. Unlike previously, when there was no minimum age for getting a credit card, CARD requires a co-signer for anyone under the age of 21. This means that college students--a prime market for many card issuers--will have a harder time getting a credit card. However, the requirement for a co-signer will be waived if a person under 21 can prove he or she is employed and is credit-worthy.

6. Credit card issuers no longer will be able to set early morning or other arbitrary deadlines for payments. Cut-off times set before 5 P.M. on the payment due date are illegal under CARD. (The time restriction is the time in the zone to which the payment is delivered.)

7. Card issuers must disclose to cardholders the consequences of making minimum-only payments. They must indicate, in writing, how long it would take to pay off the entire balance if only the minimum payment is made. Additionally, they must indicate the amount the payment would have to be if cardholders want to pay off the current balance, including interest, in 36 months.

Remember that, even though new rules are in effect, each of us still needs to consider carefully the necessity and dollar level of our credit purchases. Ask yourself, "Is this a need or a want?" "Can it wait until I have the cash?"

> **#27. If I call my credit card company and explain I am having a financial problem and will pay them in full next month, they will not charge me interest for the current month.**

REALITY

This is not true. The credit card company is not concerned about your personal financial situation. If you do not pay your bill in full by the due date, you will be charged interest. You also may be charged a late fee and may find that the interest rate on your account will go up. (Today, this late fee may be as much as $35, although the average is about $30.) The late payment also is likely to be reflected on your credit report, almost immediately.

> **#28. There is no difference between Chapter 7 and Chapter 13 bankruptcy rules. In both cases, my assets are liquidated and all my debts are wiped out.**

REALITY

Chapter 7 and Chapter 13 bankruptcy laws are decidedly different. Following is a discussion of each, along with a description of the laws related to a Chapter 11 filing.

- A Chapter 7 bankruptcy is called a "liquidation" or a "straight bankruptcy." It allows the debtor to "wipe the slate clean" and start over. In the case of a Chapter 7 bankruptcy filing, a trustee is appointed who collects the non-exempt property of the person filing for bankruptcy, sells it and distributes the proceeds to the creditors. Remaining debts are wiped away, with the exception of the following:

  1. Income taxes owed within three years of the filing date

  2. Overdue alimony and child support payments

  3. Recently made purchases for substantial amounts

  4. Student loans

  5. Properly executed contracts involving liens or titles

  Any exempt property remains the property of the filer. Because exempt property includes household goods, personal belongings and usually the filer's personal residence, Chapter 7 is a very popular form of bankruptcy, if permitted by the court.

- Bankruptcy proceedings under Chapter 13 involve the rehabilitation of the debtor to allow him or her to use future earnings to pay off creditors. It allows for a reorganization of the filer's debts with a new payment schedule. Again, a trustee is appointed to supervise the debtor's assets. A three- to five-year payment plan is made to pay from future earnings all or part of the amount owed to creditors. If you are seriously considering filing a petition of bankruptcy, you should consider a Chapter 13 filing versus Chapter 7 if there are assets you want to protect, or if you cannot pass the "means test" for a Chapter 7 filing. (See below for more information on the "means test.")

- A Chapter 11 bankruptcy is used primarily for small businesses, though select individuals may qualify. It allows the business or debtor, such as a sole proprietor, to continue normal business activities while reorganizing its finances. The theory is that an operating business that merely needs time and help with restructuring is more valuable than one that is foreclosed and has its assets liquidated.

Since the law changed in 2005, it has become much more difficult for one to qualify to file for bankruptcy. In addition, a few filers with "high" incomes no longer are allowed to file a Chapter 7 bankruptcy but are redirected to a Chapter 13 filing, under which they will have to repay at least some of their debts. To determine whether you are eligible to file for Chapter 7 bankruptcy, the law requires you to compare your current monthly income against your state's median income for a household of your size. If your income is less than or equal to your state's median income, then you can file for Chapter 7. In other words, you have to pass a "means test" to be permitted to file for Chapter 7. ("Means test" calculators are available online by going to the Web site **www.legalconsumer.com** and following the directions for the "means-test" calculator for your ZIP code.) Also, since the 2005 bankruptcy law put several very specific requirements on bankruptcy lawyers, fewer of them are accepting cases.

Finally, before being permitted to file either Chapter 7 or Chapter 13, filers must go through credit counseling sessions with an agency approved by the U. S. Trustee's Office, a branch of the Department of Justice. The purpose of the credit counseling is to help determine whether the filing is indeed the best way for you to handle the debt you have amassed. If a repayment plan is developed, it must be submitted to the bankruptcy court, along with a certificate of completion of the counseling session, before you will be allowed to file. A later component of the process is to have you attend financial literacy classes. Once completion has been certified and submitted to the court, then and only then will you get a bankruptcy discharge wiping out your debts.

#29. If I am about to file bankruptcy, I should run up my credit card accounts since, after filing, I won't have to repay them.

REALITY

This is not true. Under the current bankruptcy law, because it is so difficult to qualify for a Chapter 7 filing, it is likely you will be forced by the court to file a Chapter 13 bankruptcy petition. A Chapter 13 bankruptcy requires a full or partial repayment of outstanding debts, including credit cards. (See Reality #28) Also, remember, a bankruptcy declaration remains on your credit report for up to 10 years, depending upon which chapter you file. It negatively impacts the availability of credit, raises the cost of credit extended to you and may have a negative impact on many other aspects of your daily life.

One day, I was standing in the checkout line of my local supermarket and overheard a conversation that shocked me. The young cashier was telling the customer ahead of me that he was going on vacation and then coming back and filing for bankruptcy. I gasped and couldn't help but ask why he was going to do this. His reply was that he couldn't pay his debts, especially his student loans, so bankruptcy was his only recourse. First, I inquired as to why his student loans were so high. He told me it was because he had gone to an expensive school that he couldn't afford, to be with a friend who was going there. When I told him that student loans could not be erased by filing a petition of bankruptcy, he was astounded! That, he said, is not what "they" told him. My reply was that he was listening to the wrong people. I gave him my card and told him to call me--that I would help him sort this out, at no cost. He never called.

> #30. There is no difference between "secured" and "unsecured" credit.

REALITY

The two types of credit are decidedly different. A credit is considered "secured" when you purchase something of value that is then used to guarantee repayment, such as a car, house or boat. There is a title associated with this type of credit and the lender is listed on the title as the lien holder. It is impossible for you to sell or pledge a secured item until the lien holder signs over the title to you. Also, these are specific assets that can be taken back (repossessed) by the lender if you fail to pay. You no longer will be able to use the assets until (or unless) you bring the loan current. Also, expect slow or non-payment to negatively affect your credit rating.

On the other hand, unsecured credit does not require something tangible to guarantee the loan. Charge accounts and personal loans are examples of this type of credit. The lender usually does not repossess items purchased using unsecured credit. (The creditor does not want your towels, toaster or personal items.)

#31. The amount of credit I already have outstanding is not an important consideration in a lender's decision whether to grant me a loan.

REALITY

When trying to determine your creditworthiness, the overriding concern of any potential lender is how likely they are to be repaid. While we don't know the exact formula a particular lender uses when trying to determine whether to grant you a loan, we do know that two critical elements are the amount and type of credit you already have outstanding.

Most lenders also look at many other criteria. This includes factors such as your income level, job stability, housing stability (whether you seem to move around a lot), family size, how you have handled repaying your debts in the past and general economic conditions.

If your total debt (your existing debt plus the amount of the new loan you are seeking) compared to your income exceeds the lender's approval guidelines, then the lender may refuse to extend you the additional credit. This is called your debt-to-income ratio and is another critical factor used by a lender to determine eligibility. The lender wants to make sure the amount of credit is not so high that you are in jeopardy of not being able to repay all of your debts, especially his.

Most lenders look at what are called the "Five C's of credit analysis." These are:

1. Character (Will you pay the loan? In the past, how timely have you repaid loans?)

2. Capacity (Can you pay? Do you have the income to support repayment of the loan requested? What is the likelihood of successful repayment?)

3. Collateral (For what product or service will the loan be used? Is there additional security provided in case you default?)

4. Capital (How much of your funds have you personally invested?)

5. Conditions (What are the general economic conditions at the time the loan is requested, and what is the general purpose of the loan?)

Again, the lender wants to ensure that your personal repayment history, income and existing credit level will minimize the risk of default.

#32. There are no advantages to using credit. If I can't pay cash for my purchase, then I cannot afford it.

REALITY

This is a commonly held belief. But, there are several advantages of using credit, as long as you use it wisely.

1. Credit can be useful in times of emergency.

2. Credit can be more convenient than cash.

3. Some merchants, such as rental car companies and hotels, often require you to provide a credit card number to be able to use their services.

4. The use of credit can make it possible to make large purchases such as a car, house or major appliance.

5. Using credit can earn you rewards or miles that can be used for future purchases, dining out and/or travel.

6. Credit is often safer than cash. With a credit card, under the law, your liability is limited if the loss is reported timely. Cash can be lost or stolen with little chance that it will be recovered or replaced.

7. If there is a problem with an item purchased with a credit card, the card issuer often will help you resolve any dispute with the merchant, and may withhold the release of payment to the merchant until the matter has been resolved to your satisfaction.

8. Many credit card issuers offer a cash rebate of up to five percent of the amount purchased.

To incur the least overall cost, pay the credit card bill in its entirety by the due date, if you can. That way, you will have had the use of the creditor's money for the length of the "grace period," and it has not cost you a dime of interest. If, however, you have to pay for the purchase over an extended period of time, you may be right. Perhaps you can't afford it and should either wait until you have the funds, or choose a less expensive option that you can pay for in cash.

#33. There are no disadvantages to using credit.

REALITY

There are many disadvantages to using credit. Here are a few:

1. Credit costs money. Some credit card companies charge high interest rates when a balance is carried over from one month to the next. I am aware of rates as high as a whopping 32.99 percent!

2. The use of credit may tempt you to overspend. (Statistics show that consumers often spend as much as one-third more on purchases made with a credit card than for a similar item paid for with cash.)

3. Credit commits the use of tomorrow's income to repay today's debts.

4. Lenders report missed payments to credit bureaus, causing your credit score to be lowered.

5. Items purchased may be repossessed if payments are missed.

6. If the debt is not repaid on time, it may affect your ability to get a job, a residence or additional credit.

Again, if you must use credit to buy something that you will finance over an extended period of time, incur hefty interest rates for, or even have to pay added penalties, you may want to do without the item or wait until you can pay cash for it.

Exceptions may be what we call "big ticket items" such as a house, a car or a boat. Typically, these are items that most of us are unable to pay for with cash. You want to make sure that, for these purchases, you negotiate the best possible deal for yourself, including both the price and the cost of financing of the item.

> **#34. My credit is good. I have no debt and never have.**

REALITY

This may not be as great an idea as you think. In order for lenders to assess whether you use credit responsibly, you must show evidence of having had credit extended to you, and of having lived up to the Terms and Conditions of your contractual agreements. Thus, because you have never had credit, you may be denied the credit you seek.

You might consider opening an account in your name, using it responsibly and re-paying the debt according to the agreed terms. This will help show potential creditors that you are a reliable debtor.

> **#35. I am 24 years old, single, working and have no children. There is nothing wrong with my going to the mall to "window shop" when I have nothing else to do.**

REALITY

Unless you have a tremendous amount of discipline, this can be a financially dangerous exercise and may ultimately stand in the way of your financial security. Even if you pay cash for your purchases (as opposed to charging them), there still might be a tendency to spend money that would be better allocated someplace else or, at a minimum, saved. Temptation is often hard to resist. If you go to a mall where you are surrounded by lots of "wants" versus "needs," you may be tempted to buy unnecessary items which have little or no real value. There is an old saying that is very true: "It's better to tell your money where to go than to ask it where it went!"

If you are bored and are looking for something to do, choose an activity that does not involve the potential for spending money rather than one that might jeopardize your financial well-being.

#36. If I'm late in paying a loan, that information stays on my credit report only until I bring the delinquent debt current.

REALITY

Negative information typically stays on your credit report for many years, regardless of when the debt is cleared up. With a Chapter 13 bankruptcy, it stays on your credit report for 7 years. With a Chapter 7 declaration, it stays on for 10 years.

Negative information includes liens (tax and property), late payments, judgments, charge-offs and lawsuits. (A charge-off occurs when a lender accepts partial payment of a delinquent debt owed and "writes off" the balance. The charge-off amount is the amount of the underpayment and is usually reported to the credit bureaus.)

Credit

If you find an error on your credit report, to have it removed you must provide the credit reporting agency with written proof that the information is not valid. By law, they then have 30 days from receipt of your submission to remove any invalid information. Your submission must include the following information:

1. Your name and address

2. A description of the incorrect information

3. Support of your claim that the information is wrong

4. A request that the incorrect information be removed

All three major credit bureaus (listed in Appendix B) must remove the incorrect information. If they do not, you have the right to file a written complaint with the Federal Trade Commission in Washington, D.C. (See Appendix B for the address.)

Closed accounts stay on your credit report for 10 years, according to the folks at Fair Isaac Corp. They say that both old and closed accounts can actually help your score because they provide information about the way you have historically handled your debt. The length of your credit history accounts for 10 percent in the formula they created to calculate your FICO credit score.

You might want to re-think your belief about the impact (or lack thereof) negative credit information has on you and your non-financial life. You would be amazed at the number of seemingly non-creditors that may legitimately request access to your credit report. Following is a listing of what the law (the Fair Credit Reporting Act) defines as a "permissible purpose" for which access to your credit report may be granted by a credit bureau:

1. Credit transaction
2. Employment
3. Insurance underwriting
4. Legitimate business need
5. Court order
6. Federal jury subpoena
7. Your request

You can see from the above list that there are many non-credit-related situations in which your credit record may be an important consideration. The information contained in the credit report likely will determine whether you will be successful in being able to conduct the business you desire. Whether you will be offered a job; whether you will get insurance (and, if so, at what cost); and whether you will be extended credit are but a few examples of why your credit report is so important.

One of my students was very upset because her poor credit history was hampering her ability to get a job. She had received three job offers and each was withdrawn after the potential employer examined her credit report. She was applying for a job as a security officer.

There are many other potential employment situations where your credit history can come back to haunt you. For example, if you have recently filed for bankruptcy, you may not be able to get or keep a security clearance. (Clearance is about your ability to be trusted with access to classified information or other resources/assets.) Bad credit, some potential employers believe, may make you an easy bribe target. The concern is that security lapses may be more likely to happen if a person is desperate for money.

A lot depends upon the agency or company involved, the amount of time that has passed since your bankruptcy, your current credit status and the type of clearance needed. So, again, you can see how maintaining a good, clean credit history can have a big impact on your life.

> **#37. All lenders look at credit the same way. Therefore, if I can't get credit from one lender because of negative information on my credit report, there is no point in trying another.**

REALITY

First, "all lenders are not created equal." Lenders use different guidelines for assessing applicant creditworthiness. Because you probably will never know the exact criteria a lender uses, if you get turned down by one lender, always try another. Although the terms and conditions might be less favorable than those of the preferred lender, a second lender might be willing to take a chance on you. You may find that some amount of credit may be granted even though it could be for a shorter term, at a higher interest rate or for a lesser amount.

One class participant admittedly had an especially bad credit history. She was in the market for a used car but was having trouble finding anyone willing to extend her credit. Finally, she found a willing lender but at a very high cost. The quoted interest rate was a whopping 24 percent! She asked me what I thought she should do. My recommendation? BMW--bus, metro or walk! I think she took my suggestion. That was an exorbitant interest rate and the term of the loan was seven years, which probably was longer than the life expectancy of the used car she was considering.

#38. If my credit is bad, I can pay someone to quickly "fix" my credit and remove all negative information from my credit report.

REALITY

This is a myth that is quite widespread, but has no basis in fact. The following are universal truths about credit repair:

1. No one can have accurate information removed from your credit report; not even you!

2. If you have had credit problems in the past, it can take years to repair your credit legitimately.

3. No one can create a new identity for you. Each of us gets one and only one Social Security number. Even if someone offers to get an EIN (employer identification number) for you, it is tied to your Social Security number. Plus, under the credit repair statutes, changing your identity to avoid debt repayment is against the law.

4. You can order your own credit report. You are legally entitled to one free credit report a year from each of the three major credit reporting agencies listed in Appendix B. I recommend ordering one every four months from a different agency to have a general idea, all year, about what is in your credit report. If you see

errors on your credit report, you can submit the supporting documentation to the credit bureau yourself and request that the appropriate corrections be made. By law, the agencies have 30 days to remove negative information when they receive documentation that clearly indicates that the information on your credit report is incorrect. If they do not cooperate, you may submit a written complaint to the Federal Trade Commission in Washington, D.C. (See Appendix B for the address.)

Some credit repair clinics are legitimate; but, many are not. Most do nothing for you that you cannot do for yourself. You can call creditors to renegotiate payment schedules and try to get lower credit payoff amounts. Also, beware of any credit-related entity that advertises on trees, stop signs or traffic signals. Legitimate businesses do not advertise that way! "The number of complaints the states have received against debt-relief companies, particularly debt-settlement companies, has been consistently rising and has more than doubled since 2007," according to an October 23, 2009 letter from 40 states attorneys general to the Federal Trade Commission.

If you find you need help, there are several organizations you can contact that have no motive other than to help you work through your financial distress. The National Foundation for Credit Counseling (NFCC), one of the largest non-profit credit counseling organizations in the country, is one such entity. It offers consumers both financial education and counseling services. Their web address is **www.nfcc.org**. Another is Operation Hope, Inc. (HOPE), a provider of financial literacy and economic empowerment programs. HOPE has developed a series of programs to provide free financial education to youths and adults nationwide. Check your local listing for offices in your area.

> **#39. If I co-sign for a loan for a friend or family member and they fail to repay the loan according to the terms of the agreement, I won't be held responsible for the unpaid balance.**

REALITY

This is another myth that is quite widespread and often misunderstood. First of all, remember that your friend or relative has asked you to co-sign because, based upon their stand-alone credit record, they have been denied credit. If a professional lender has turned your friend or relative down, consider that it probably is for good reason and is something you should not take lightly. (Ask yourself why you think they will repay this loan--in both your names--in a timely fashion, if they did not pay back money borrowed in their name alone.)

In almost all states, if the borrower misses a payment, by law, the lender immediately can (and usually will) turn to the co-signer without even trying to collect from the borrower. Such a delinquency negatively affects your credit rating just as though you were the original borrower and will show up as a liability on your credit record. This could prevent you from getting credit for yourself in the future. In addition to being required to bring the payments current, you could be assessed late fees, have your wages garnished and/or be sued (and even be assessed legal fees).

The bottom line is that you should never co-sign for any loan that you are not able and willing to repay. You should treat any loan as though you were borrowing the money yourself. Do not co-sign away your good credit!

Despite the risks outlined above, there still may come a time when you want to or have to co-sign for a loan. Perhaps one of your children, a close friend or a family member needs help in establishing credit. Just make sure you do the following before you co-sign:

1. Be certain you can afford to repay the loan if called upon to do so.

2. Be aware that your own credit rating may be affected if the loan goes into default.

3. Recognize that you may be prohibited from getting credit approved for yourself because of having your name on this outstanding loan.

4. Understand that if sued because of a default, you may lose some of your own valuable items as the lender tries to collect.

5. Completely read the loan documents (and get a copy).

6. Fully comprehend your duties and rights as a co-signer.

Remember, adding your name to someone else's debt is taking on a very serious financial responsibility. If the lender did not have doubts about the borrower's ability or willingness to repay the loan, no co-signer would have been required. Mimi would remind you, **"There is none so blind as he who will not see."** Also, she would tell you to **"Look deep before you leap!"**

#40. I need a relatively small amount of money quickly and cannot find a regular lender to make me a loan. Since I can prove I have a job, can't I just go to a "payday lender" or to a "title loan" company and get the same terms I would get from a bank or credit union?

REALITY

"Payday lenders" are lenders who charge exorbitant fees to people who need money quickly and can't get a loan from a more mainstream lender like a bank or credit union. Their only two requirements are that you have a job and a checking account. These lenders advance you money, theoretically, until your next payday.

Here is how these loans work. The payday lender writes you a check for the amount of the loan. You give the lender a check written on your checking account for the amount of the loan, plus fees. The lender then holds your check until your next payday at which time, by agreement, your check is deposited or cashed. Statistics show the average payday loan is renewed seven times with just the interest being paid (not the principal amount borrowed), and can result in interest rates of 300 percent or higher, plus fees!

One client is a single female with no children who makes $85,000 per year. Her expenses were so far out of proportion to her income that she practically lived off payday loans. When we met, she had five of them. Three were for $300; one was for $250; and one was for $350 for a total of $1,500--all with different payday lenders. Every payday, she merely paid each lender a 30 percent fee ($450 in total) and rolled over the principal amounts. Most of her lenders would not accept partial repayment of the principal. So, unless she had the entire $250, $300 or $350, some would only accept the interest and another two-week loan agreement. She rolled these loans over six times. By the time she was done, she had paid the $450 fee 6 times, plus the principal amount, for a total of $4,200 to borrow $1,500 for about 12 weeks!

Similarly, title loans are another way for those who need money to get it quickly. These loans are made to people who can prove they are the registered owner of a vehicle that has no loan on it. The lenders who work in this arena will lend you up to 50 percent of the Black Book value of your car. (The Black Book value is the auction value and is much less than the Blue Book value.) These lenders want to be able to sell your car quickly and still come out whole, should you default on the loan. When you go to this type of lender, you must have a clean and clear title. All owners listed on the title must come in and sign over the title, and you must bring a spare key! The latter allows the lender to repossess your car easily in the event you do not repay the loan. Their rates are almost as high as those of the payday lenders mentioned above.

My advice to you is to avoid these types of loans, and find another source for your short-term cash needs. Typically, banks and credit unions offer rates that are much lower than those of payday and title lenders. You should try these alternatives before seeking out the more expensive ones.

> **#41. Opening a new charge account to take advantage of in-store offerings that give you a 10 to 20 percent discount on first-day purchases is always a good idea since it saves you money.**

REALITY

According to Fair Isaac Corp., the people who developed the FICO credit scoring formula used by most creditors, 10 percent of your credit score is affected by the number of requests for new credit that you have. The more inquiries into your credit history, the more it looks like you are constantly searching for new credit. Then, once you open this new account, the scoring model sees that as more "credit opportunity." This results in a lower credit score.

Ask yourself whether 10 to 20 percent off on your purchase is worth the hit to your credit score. In most cases, especially where there are small purchases being made, it isn't. So, be smart. Decline those offers unless the discount represents a significant amount of money to you.

> **#42. All debts are the same. The type doesn't matter.**

REALITY

For purposes of computing your credit score, the type of debt you have matters greatly. According to Fair Isaac Corp., the owner of the FICO credit scoring model, the type of debt you have accounts for 10 percent of your credit score. Debt types include consumer installment loans (automobile, computer and furniture), revolving credit (credit cards), home loans (home purchase, refinance and equity) and student loans.

Most financial experts talk about "good" debt and "bad" debt. "Good" debt is usually defined as debt you incur to buy something that either increases in value or has the potential of making you money. Examples are residential real estate, student loans and some investments.

On the other hand, "bad" debt is incurred to purchase things that do not either increase in value or make you money. Credit card debt is the major type of "bad" debt that most of us incur. We use our credit cards for things such as food and entertainment, vacations and clothing. Of course, if you have no food or clothes, then you might have to incur some "bad" debt to survive, but every effort should be made to pay it off as soon as possible so you do not incur finance charges. Though we don't know for sure, it is believed that "bad" debt more negatively impacts your credit score than "good" debt.

#43. Missing a couple of credit card payments will not hurt my credit score, especially if it doesn't happen that often.

REALITY

When you owe a debt, your lender, rightfully, expects to be repaid. Missed payments are reported to the credit bureaus (often, as soon as they happen) and negatively affect your credit score. Nothing, except filing for bankruptcy, hurts your credit score more than failing to pay at least the minimum required on your accounts. Not doing so is a sign to the credit-rating agencies that you are having trouble paying your debts. Potential creditors will see any delinquencies when they pull your credit report. Many, after seeing the negative marks, will not extend you credit.

One client proudly sported an 810 credit score. An incorrect report of a single delinquency caused her score to be lowered to 675—over 125 points! Fortunately, after great effort on her part, she was able to get it corrected and to have her score restored.

#44. Having unpaid library and parking fines, or past-due homeowner assessments won't hurt my credit score since they do not represent real "debt."

REALITY

Yes, it can, depending upon where you live. Many municipalities and other government entities, and homeowner associations are starting to report delinquencies to the three credit-reporting agencies. If so, this information will indeed negatively impact your credit score (maybe, for years to come). For best results, pay any fines and assessments in a timely fashion to keep them from showing up on your credit report.

CHAPTER 5

ESTATE PLANNING

ESTATE PLANNING

Mimi-isms:

"Thrift in a man is never appreciated more
than when his Will is read."

"Don't count your chickens before they hatch."

#45. Only rich people need an estate plan.

REALITY

First, let me define estate planning. Estate planning is a process you and your advisors go through to set up legally effective arrangements regarding how you want your assets distributed during your lifetime and after your death. Your estate plan includes who you want to oversee the distribution and control of your assets, as well as make decisions regarding your care in the event of your death or serious disability.

Who should have an estate plan? You should if any or all of the following apply to you:

1. You have minor or incapacitated children or adults for whom you are responsible.

2. You have assets.

3. You want to define your own healthcare treatment, if you become incapacitated.

Typically, some combination of the following five documents is included in an estate plan:

1. Will (or "Last Will and Testament") to transfer property you hold in your name to the person(s) you want to have it. It also names an executor or personal representative as the person you designate to carry out your wishes and names a guardian for your dependent children. If you do not set out this direction, the state

in which you are a legal resident will determine the guardian. It may not be the person you would have chosen.

2. "Durable Power of Attorney for Health Care" (also called a "Health Care Proxy" or "Advance Health Care Directive") to appoint someone to make healthcare treatment decisions for you if you cannot make them for yourself.

3. "Living Will" to direct your doctors and hospital regarding providing or stopping medical treatment should you become permanently incapacitated.

4. "Durable Power of Attorney" to appoint someone to act on your behalf to handle your legal and financial matters, if you are no longer able to do so.

5. "Living Trust" to hold legal title and provide a mechanism to manage your property. You can select the person you want, including yourself, to serve as trustee to carry out your instructions. Also, you usually select a successor trustee to act as your representative if something happens to you. Unlike a Will, a trust can carry on after your death.

Not having an estate plan (including a Will) means having the state where you live make major decisions regarding matters such as the guardianship of your minor or incapacitated children, distribution of your assets, and your healthcare, should you become incapacitated or die. Without a Will, you will be deemed to have died "intestate." (Every state has "laws of intestacy" which determine the distribution of your assets upon your death as well as who gets to make healthcare decisions for you if/when you cannot make them for yourself.)

Your estate plan not only directs the distribution of your personal assets and property, but also, it helps make your wishes known about your finances and healthcare, should you become incapacitated. You do not have to be wealthy to plan for an orderly transition.

Do you remember the Terri Schiavo case several years ago involving the parents of a young woman who had not done her estate planning? They were fighting the husband of their daughter, who had been in a comatose state for several years, because he wanted to remove her life-sustaining feeding tube.

After a lengthy battle including involvement of the U.S. Congress, the court ultimately sided with Ms. Schiavo's husband and her life support was removed. She died shortly thereafter from the effects of dehydration. If she had had a properly executed "Durable Power of Attorney for Health Care," we all would have been spared the agony of such a public debate.

A Will doesn't have to be expensive. Do-it-yourself software programs like WillMaker by Quicken, and those prepared by using templates found on **www.legalzoom.com**, are adequate for a basic Will. However, if your situation is complex, then it would be wise for you to consult an estate planning attorney.

> #### #46. With the creation of a living trust, I lose control over any assets I place in the name of the trust.

REALITY

First, let me define the term "trust." A trust is a legal entity represented by a legal document in which one person, the *trustee*, holds property for the benefit of another, the *beneficiary*. The property can be any kind of real or personal property.

Trusts fall into two main categories—"revocable" and "irrevocable." If a trust is revocable, the trust can be changed.   If a trust is irrevocable, the trust cannot be changed. A "living trust" is a widely known document that is created during your lifetime; it is familiar to and accepted by financial institutions and the legal community.

When a " revocable living trust" is created, most property owners name themselves as trustee. This gives you the power to retain control over trust assets just as you did before you created the trust. Also, you can change the provisions of your trust at any time. A "successor trustee" is named to act on your behalf in the event of your incapacity or death. If you become disabled, then the "successor trustee" steps in to manage your assets according to the provisions you set forth in the trust. If you become incapacitated without a "living trust" or a power of attorney, then a state court will appoint a conservator to manage your affairs and will name a guardian for your dependents, if you have any.

When an "irrevocable living trust" is created, you, the property owner, voluntarily relinquish control of the trust's assets, and you cannot make further changes regarding trust beneficiaries. The assets are completely controlled by the named trustee. Such a trust is often created as an estate tax avoidance mechanism to remove assets from an individual's estate, if the estate's value is approaching the congressionally-defined per-person limit. Once you shift assets away from your ownership with this type of trust, there are fewer assets for the IRS to tax.

One reason individuals establish trusts is to keep their assets from going through the very public, costly and time-consuming court process called probate--a legal process through which property ownership is transferred from the decedent to the designated heir. Probate can cost as much as 10 percent of the assets going through the process and can take as long as three years, depending upon the size and complexity of the probate estate.

Remember, once you set up a trust, you must re-title the assets you want transferred into the trust in the name of the trust. Otherwise, you will have an empty trust and the document will have no value.

The value of all trust assets is included in the deceased's estate for estate tax purposes. For 2010, the law decreed no federal estate taxes due, regardless of the size of the estate. For 2011 and beyond, estate taxes are assessed on estates with values of $1.0 million or more and the top tax rate is 45 percent.

> *#47. Most baby boomers can expect to get very large*
> *inheritances from their parents.*

REALITY

Despite predictions of a massive transfer of wealth between generations, many baby boomers might find they will get limited inheritances from their parents. While economists and financial professionals cannot agree on the total amount this generation and their offspring actually might inherit, they do agree that the amount transferred is likely to be far less than expected and that many heirs will end up disappointed.

According to a Federal Reserve Board study done several years ago, the median inheritance baby boomers received was just under $50,000. However, most survey responders (83 percent) indicated they had received no money to date. These low inheritances are smaller than expected due, in part, to payment of estate taxes and charitable bequests outlined in Wills. Increasing life spans, rising healthcare and nursing home costs, and the conversion of lump-sum pensions to an annuity all are impacting baby boomers' inheritance size.

Reverse mortgages also are diminishing expected inheritances. In addition, lifetime gifts to family members and friends, and expenditures on oneself mean there might be less left over for heirs.

If you are among the fortunate 20 percent or so who have received or expect to get an inheritance, don't waste the money by it spending frivolously or by making risky financial moves. Instead, depending upon your financial situation, use it to pay down debts or to increase your own assets so you can live more comfortably in retirement.

> *#48. My heirs can avoid the cost of probate by handling the settlement of my estate themselves, without the assistance of the court.*

REALITY

It is the probate court that has jurisdiction with respect to Wills and intestacies (dying without a Will). When a person dies, the executor of the estate files the Will with the local court, giving the court jurisdiction to enforce the document. (This is called "filing the Will for probate.") The process of "probating" the Will involves recognition by the court of the executor named in the Will, or appointment of an administrator if none has been named; filing proper reports and papers as required by law; determining the validity of the Will, if contested; and the distribution and final settling of the estate under the supervision of the court. This cannot be done outside of the court process.

After your death, the executor of your estate must appear before the court in the jurisdiction in which you lived, with your original Will to prove it is valid In other words, the executor must prove that you really did sign the Will, that you were not acting under duress or undue influence, and that you were competent at the time you signed the Will. As mentioned above, this is a legal proceeding and cannot be done outside of the court environment.

#49. The provisions of a Will override the actual way in which assets, especially real estate, are distributed.

REALITY

This is not true. For example, a written Will has no affect on any assets the deceased held with another person in "joint tenancy with rights of survivorship." For example, if a widow holds title to a property in joint tenancy with one offspring and the Will provides for sale of the property with equal distribution of the proceeds to each of four surviving children, there will be no distribution to three of the children. The house automatically goes to the named "joint tenant" and the other offspring will get nothing unless the sibling/owner chooses to share with them. The only possible way to achieve the mother's wishes is for the executor to ask the sibling/owner to sign a "quit claim deed," thereby relinquishing ownership in the property. Only then will that provision of the Will be honored.

The same is true for bank accounts, life insurance, investment accounts or any other asset where there is a named beneficiary. They cannot be "Will-ed" away, meaning they cannot be left in the Will to someone else. This is one of the reasons it is critical that beneficiary designations be kept up-to-date. There have been many stories where a deceased's assets went to an unintended recipient such as an ex-spouse, former friend or estranged child. Because the deceased "forgot" to update his or her beneficiary designation, the named beneficiary, by law, was deemed the rightful owner.

> **#50. To ensure my minor child inherits my house, I should leave my house, in my Will, to that child.**

REALITY:

In most states, the age of majority is 18 years. So, you do not want to leave your house to a minor. Minors cannot convey property or legally sign contracts. Therefore, you should make sure you name a trustee in your Will who will hold title for the benefit of your minor child(ren) until at least the age of majority or some other pre-set age you have defined. Regardless of the age you set, it must be spelled out in the Will.

Be aware that leaving a house to a child or to anyone else in a Will, rather than titling the house in the name of your *revocable living trust,* will not lead to probate avoidance. (Probate is the legal process assets must go through to change the name of the titleholder to your designated beneficiary or to the beneficiary the state assigns if you have no Will.) Titling the house in the name of your trust, with you as trustee and a named successor trustee, will avoid probate and the associated probate costs of 4.5 to 10.0 percent of the value of the probate assets as well as delays of up to three years, depending upon the jurisdiction where the probate process occurs and the size and complexity of the probate estate.

In one case I know of, a mother added her minor child's name to her property when her husband died because she wanted to ensure that he would always have a place to live. When that child was a teenager, the mother, recently remarried, wanted to sell the house and the court had to become involved because one of the owners of the house, her son, was still a minor. The court-appointed representative determined that the best use of the minor child's equity in the home was to place it in a college fund. This meant the mother did not have the full amount she anticipated to use toward the purchase of a new home.

> **#51. If I become incapacitated and cannot make medical decisions for myself, the court will automatically designate my parents to make them for me.**

REALITY

A document called an "Advance Health Care Directive" lays out your medical care preferences under specific circumstances as well as who you want to make these decisions on your behalf when you can't. If you become medically unable to make decisions about your care without benefit of such a document, then the court will allow your legal next-of-kin to make medical decisions on your behalf. If married, this will most likely be your spouse. If unmarried, this probably will be your parents, if they are still alive. After that, each state's law determines the decision maker.

> **#52. I cannot get my 98-year-old mother, who has a common-law husband of 25 years, to draw up a Will. I say he has no legal rights to my mother's estate when she passes.**

REALITY

Many states have laws making it impossible to disinherit the surviving spouse completely without a prenuptial or cohabitation agreement. Usually, a common-law marriage counts as long as the surviving spouse can prove they presented themselves as a married couple.

If your mother dies without a Will, she will die "intestate," and the control and distribution of her assets will pass to the probate court in the state in which she and her common-law husband live. To have a valid claim, he will have to file a petition in probate court within six months after probate is opened. If they have been "married" for at least 10 years, he may be legally entitled to as much as half of her estate. It is very likely the court will award him some portion of your mother's estate. The best thing to do is to, again, try to convince her to have a valid Will drawn up and properly witnessed. This will help limit the confusion surrounding who gets what when she passes.

#53. It is a good decision to name minor children as beneficiaries of a 401(k) or an Individual Retirement Account (IRA).

REALITY

Many parents have substantial assets in their retirement accounts. Most minors do not have the financial savvy to handle large amounts of money, especially if given to them in a lump sum. Therefore, anyone who has minor children should consider having a Will to direct distribution of their assets, combined with an "age terminating trust" with the management of the money handled by either their executor or a named trustee, such as a financial institution. Such a trust can ensure that children don't receive too much money at too young an age. For example, one could direct that a third of one's assets be given to them at age 21; another third at age 25; and the balance at age 30. In this example, the trust is emptied when the beneficiary turns 30--thus, the name, "age terminating trust."

One of my colleagues had a client who, at age 18, was scheduled to receive $1.6 million from an *irrevocable* trust set up by her grandfather. There was no provision for a later distribution and no one, not her parents, not even the trustee, could change the terms of the trust since it was an *irrevocable* trust. The money would become legally hers at age 18, and there was nothing anyone could do about it. You can imagine how many "friends" she had just waiting for a shopping spree.

#54. If I die before I start receiving Social Security benefits, my survivors are not eligible to receive any payments. Those benefits are "lost" forever.

REALITY

Some of the Social Security taxes you pay go toward providing "survivor's benefits" for certain members of your family. Covered are widows and widowers, including those divorced but un-remarried; dependent children; and parents. A beneficiary should apply for survivor benefits promptly because, in some cases, benefits are paid only from the time one files and may not be retroactive.

Your widow or widower can receive full benefits at age 65 or older if born before January 2, 1940, or reduced benefits as early as age 60. For widows and widowers born after January 2, 1940, depending upon the actual year of their birth, the age for receiving full benefits has increased from age 65 to as much as age 67. However, a <u>disabled</u> widow or widower can get benefits as early as age 50.

Your surviving spouse can receive benefits at any age if he or she takes care of your child who is entitled to a child's benefit and is age 16 or younger. This is also true if the surviving spouse cares for a disabled child. Your unmarried children who are under age 18 (or up to age 19 if they are attending elementary or secondary school full time) also are eligible to receive benefits. Under certain circumstances, stepchildren, adopted children and grandchildren also qualify for benefits.

Finally, your dependent parents may receive benefits if they are 62 or older. For your parents to qualify as dependents, they must be able to prove that you, at the time of your death, provided at least 50 percent of their support. In addition, your parent cannot be entitled to his or her own higher Social Security benefit; must file a claim within two years of your death; and, if single, cannot have remarried since your death.

> **#55. If my spouse dies, any monies owed him will be sent to me automatically by the agency that owes the money.**

REALITY

After the death of a loved one, financial management issues will require a lot of your attention. You may choose to handle these matters yourself, or you may seek the assistance of a financial advisor. Upon the passing of your spouse, it will be your responsibility to identify and to notify institutions that may owe you money. This includes entities such as insurance companies, current or even prior employer(s), the Social Security Administration, financial institutions and your spouse's attorney.

Be sure to have gathered all the relevant documents when you approach these organizations since they will want both proof of your relationship to the deceased and proof of death. (Make at least 20 copies of the death certificate.) Such documents should include marriage and death certificates, the deceased's Social Security number, the original of the deceased's Will, deeds to any jointly owned real property, the last two years' tax returns and a complete list of assets.

#56. From a tax perspective, I should give my real estate to my heirs now rather than making them wait to inherit it.

REALITY

This was a true statement until 2010. Prior to 2010, property owned by a decedent at the time of death had its tax basis changed from what the decedent's basis was to its fair market value at the time of his/her death (or six months later) - whichever was higher. (This is commonly referred to as a "step up in basis.") For the year 2010 - and only that year - the law was changed to 'whichever is lower'. This change, in general, will cost inheritors of decedents who die in 2010 more taxes, especially those inheriting real estate. However, it is expected that legislators will reverse this law during 2010 and bring back the "stepped-up basis" (corresponding to 'whichever is greater') that estate property, historically, has received. (This change in the law came from the Economic Growth and Tax Relief Reconciliation Act of 2001. It provided for the repeal of the law that gave the 'whichever was greater' provision at death in exchange for the change in tax basis for those dying after 2009. The 2001 law also eliminated all estate taxation for 2010 because, at the time, the hope was that we wouldn't need monies from the estate tax after 2009.)

For purposes of the rest of this discussion, let's assume that the law indeed will be changed back to the "whichever is higher" provision. In that case, unless you are very wealthy and your estate far exceeds the amount of the federal exclusion for gift tax purposes ($1 million in one's lifetime), where taxes are concerned, it may be more beneficial to your heirs to wait until after your death to receive the real property. In that case, under the "whichever is higher" provision, inheriting property versus receiving it as a gift has a very valuable tax advantage, especially if the property has greatly increased in value since the time of its original purchase. Typically, a house owned by a decedent at his/her death has a tax basis that is considerably less than its fair market value at that time. When a gift is given while you are alive, the property's original cost basis transfers to the gift recipient. (In the case of real estate, the original cost basis equals the original purchase price of the property, plus capital improvements.) However, with a "step up in basis," if your heir sold the house right away, at its fair market value, there would be no capital gains tax to be paid since the selling price equaled its tax basis (which had been "stepped up" to the fair market value). Capital gains taxes are assessed on the difference between the selling price plus costs associated with the sale, and the beneficiary's basis in the property.

Under the old law, if your heirs received the property as a gift during your lifetime, the tax bite would be much larger because they would have to assume your low basis in the property and must pay capital gains taxes on the difference between that low amount and the selling price. On the other hand, if your heirs inherit the property, then they only would be assessed taxes on the difference between the higher "stepped-up basis" plus selling costs, and the selling price.

A simple example might help show the distinction. Suppose your grandmother purchased a house for $25,000 many years ago. Grandma just passed and you have decided to sell what is now your house which has a "date of death value" of $400,000. Someone has offered to buy it from you for $400,000.

Let's look at the tax implications of each of the two scenarios described above, under the old law. In the first case, grandma adds your name to her title while she is still alive; in the second case, she leaves the home to you in her Will.

- Case I Tax Computation--Your name is **added** to the title during grandma's lifetime:

Your "basis" in the property is calculated by adding together grandma's purchase price of $25,000; plus improvements over the years amounting to $75,000; plus $40,000 in costs associated with selling the house, including real estate commissions, for a total of $140,000.

Capital gains taxes will be owed on the difference between your selling price of the house ($400,000) and your basis ($140,000) for a total difference of $260,000 ($400,000-$140,000). At an average rate of 15 percent, your federal capital gains taxes alone will be about $39,000. (State taxes must be calculated and paid separately, if applicable.)

- Case II Tax Computation--The house is **left** to you in grandma's Will:

Again, under the old law, for purposes of calculating capital gains taxes, inherited property receives a "step up in basis" which is an increase to its value on grandma's date of death or six months later, whichever you choose. Let's say your basis in the property is "stepped up" to $400,000--the value on the day grandma died. Capital gains taxes are owed on the difference between your selling price of the house ($400,000) and your new basis ($400,000) for a total of difference of $0 ($400,000 minus $400,000). At an average rate of 15 percent, your federal capital gains taxes alone will be $0! There will be no state taxes owed either. (Selling costs are not relevant here because your basis already is equal to the selling price.)

As you can see, inheriting property rather than having it gifted during the benefactor's lifetime, in this case, is a much better financial alternative. Even considering state and local taxes, the advantage is still on the side of inheriting property, unless the giver is extremely wealthy and has to consider added gift and estate taxes. Let's hope the 'whichever is lower law' indeed will be reversed.

#57. It is not possible to refuse an unwanted inheritance.

REALITY:

You might wonder why someone would want to do so. For a variety of reasons, accepting such a legacy might result in financial complications, thus leading some to renounce their rights. For example, if you have an estate valued at more than the then-current federal estate-tax-free exclusion amount, you may have already planned for an estate of a certain size. The addition of more assets could lead to a much worsened tax situation for your heirs.

Here's another example. Your favorite aunt has left you her timeshare property in South Carolina. You have no interest in using it and do not want to be stuck with having to pay the annual maintenance fee. Also, you have heard timeshares are almost impossible to sell or to give away to charity. You, therefore, decide to "disclaim" the inheritance.

To accommodate situations like these and others, there is a provision in the law that allows a beneficiary to disclaim unwanted assets. However, the following strict rules must be adhered to:

1. The disclaimer must be in writing to the executor.

2. It must be made within nine months after the decedent's death.

3. As the named heir, you must not have accepted any benefits from the disclaimed property.

4. You may have no say in directing where the disclaimed property will go.

5. Your disclaimer is irrevocable (cannot be changed).

So, you can see, it is possible to "disclaim" an unwanted inheritance. However, it just must be done in accordance within the law's provisions.

> **#58. A "Family Love Letter," which spells out my desires upon my death, is a legally enforceable document.**

REALITY

A "Family Love Letter" is a gift of time, love and clarity. It is a document you might create, either in longhand or typed, that describes what you want to happen to your assets and provides a roadmap of where vital information is kept.

Unlike a Will, a "Family Love Letter" is not a legally enforceable document. Its chief purpose is to provide clarity about your wishes in a number of different areas. It may contain information about things like passwords, codes to safes, contact information for financial service providers, burial instructions, and who you want to get specific assets. It is intended to help avoid family misunderstandings and disagreements, and to provide explanations for the decisions you made.

However, a "Family Love Letter" is not a Will substitute. If there is no legal Will, you will be determined to have died "intestate" (without a Will), and your state's laws of intestacy will apply. This means there is a high likelihood your assets will have to go through the court process known as probate before they can be distributed to your heirs. Dying "intestate" also could mean the people who you identified in your Family Love Letter as the ones you want to get your assets may not actually get them, since your state's order of distribution will prevail.

My advice--make a valid Will. That should help minimize the disagreements and confusion.

Mimi, Money and Me

CHAPTER 6

REAL ESTATE

REAL ESTATE

Mimi-isms

"A man's home is his castle."

"The sun's gonna shine in my backyard someday."

"Home is where the heart is."[4]

"There's no place like home."

---

[4] Pliny the Elder

#59. A law still exists that provides a one-time capital gains exclusion of $125,000 for home sellers 55 and older.

REALITY

There no longer is an "over 55" tax rule that goes into effect when a home is sold. That law was superseded by Internal Revenue Code 121, which is a tax exemption of up to $250,000 for any owner who sells a personal residence in which he or she was a full-time occupant for at least 24 of the 60 months before the sale. Each named titleholder who meets this requirement is eligible for the capital gains exemption.

This exemption can only be used once every 24 months, with special exemptions for military and work-related moves. IRC 121 (d)(9) is a special military and Foreign Service exception which extends the occupancy test to 10 years from 60 months. However, the 24-month occupancy test still must be met to get the full exemption amount. The amount may be pro-rated for an occupancy period of less than 24 months. Also, it is possible to obtain a pro-rated exemption for sales when one has a medical or work-related reason.

#60. The amount of property taxes I can deduct on my tax return is equal to the amount I paid into the escrow account along with my mortgage payment.

REALITY

An escrow account is an account created by the mortgage lender to retain the mortgage holder's monthly tax and insurance premium payments. Each month, the homeowner deposits one-twelfth of the estimated annual insurance premium and tax amount owed. The mortgage lender collects these amounts, receives the actual bills, and then pays the insurance company and taxing authorities the amounts due. Both Federal Housing Authority (FHA) and Department of Veterans Affairs (VA) loans require escrow accounts. Also, many homeowners prefer to have such accounts rather than pay these expenses themselves, in lump sums.

The amount you can deduct on your tax return is the amount actually paid by the mortgage lender on your behalf. It is not necessarily equal to the payments you made. (The actual bill amount may be different than your monthly escrow payments, leaving you with a surplus or shortfall in your escrow account.) Each January, your mortgage lender must send you an IRS Form 1098 that shows the actual tax amount paid on your behalf. This is the amount you can deduct on your tax return for the prior year.

#61. There is no downside to a "cash-out refi" if I need extra cash to pay expenses.

REALITY

The term "cash out refi" refers to the act of refinancing and taking equity out of your home. It is the refinancing of a mortgage in which the new principal exceeds the outstanding principal owed on the home. Fannie Mae, one of the largest providers of mortgage money, estimated that in the early-to-mid 2000s, 4 out of every 5 re-financings were "cash-out refi's."

Funds are used for a multitude of reasons, such as to pay off credit card debt, home improvements, college costs, travel and other expenses. However, when market values decline, many homeowners become what is known as "under water," meaning they owe more on their home than its current market value, so fewer are able to execute a "cash-out refi." (Today, no legitimate lender will loan you more than the current market value of your home.)

There are both positives and negatives to a "cash-out re-fi." On the positive side, such re-financings have been relatively easy to obtain and tend to carry lower interest rates than either second mortgages or personal loans. Lenders tend to get more restrictive when home values decline. But, if you have sufficient equity in your home and have very good credit, such loans usually are available. Also, with a "cash-out refi," you take out the entire approved amount at once.

On the negative side, there may be several disadvantages to a "cash-out re-fi." First, your payments immediately reflect that larger loan amount. (Can you handle the larger payment?) Second, with a seemingly large, lump sum in your hands, you may have a tendency to spend more than you would if you had taken small increments. Third, you are carrying more debt secured by your house which puts your most important asset at greater risk if you lose your job or run into financial difficulties. Fourth, refinancing costs are usually higher than home equity lines of credit (HELOCs) as discussed below in Reality #62. However, there is no risk of you not being able to take out the full amount you need because the lender has shut off your source of funds, as might be the case with a HELOC.

#62. Home equity lines of credit (HELOCs) are preferable to "cash-out refi's."

REALITY

There are a number of good reasons to consider home equity lines of credit (HELOCs) if you need additional cash. First, repayment does not begin until you actually "draw down" on the line. Second, once you have been approved for the loan, the timing of the use of the line is within your control. Your payment amount, including interest, totally depends upon how much of the line (up to its maximum) you use and when. Third, many financial institutions allow you the option of converting a variable-rate home equity line of credit into a fixed-rate loan, at your option, if you can prove you are able to repay the loan priced this way. (With variable-rate loans, the interest rate changes over the term of the loan according to some pre-set, contractually agreed upon formula. With fixed-rate loans, the interest rate is constant throughout the term of the loan.)

A disadvantage of a HELOC is when home values decline significantly, many lenders "cap" home equity lines and prohibit borrowers from drawing down amounts in excess of the "cap." This can be a problem, particularly for borrowers in the middle of a big project they are paying for in stages, such as a major renovation or payment of higher education costs.

#63. Several years ago, my father gave me his house which I now want to sell. It has significantly increased in value. I can use the market value of the property on the date of sale as my basis in the house.

REALITY

No, you cannot. For the purpose of calculating the amount of your capital gain, you must take over your father's basis in the property, which may be very low. (His basis is his actual purchase price plus the cost of any capital improvements he made during his lifetime.) The market value on the date you sell the house is not a factor in determining your basis.

Unless the property is your principal residence and you have owned and occupied it for at least 24 of the last 60 months before the actual sale (so you can qualify for the $250,000 exemption described in Reality #59 above), you must pay taxes on the full amount of your profit on the sale. The amount of your profit is equal to the amount you sell the house for, minus your "adjusted cost basis." (The adjusted cost basis equals the sum of your father's purchase price, capital improvements made by your father or you, real estate commissions and any other selling costs paid by you.)

Again, if this property has been your residence for at least 24 of the past 60 months, then the first $250,000 of profit is exempt from capital gains taxes. Since this exclusion can represent a significant amount of money, sellers who are not currently living in a property they want to sell (or have not lived in it within the past 60 months) have been known to move into it for the minimum amount of time required to qualify for the exclusion.

#64. If I add someone's name to the title to my home, this will trigger a new "stepped-up basis" for the home.

REALITY

No, it will not. When you add an individual's name to your property versus having them inherit it, they assume your basis in the property. (Your basis in the property is defined as the original purchase price plus any capital improvements made during your period of ownership.)

For purposes of calculating the amount of capital gains tax they will owe when they decide to sell the property, historically it has been much more advantageous for a loved one to inherit the property than to have their name added to it, especially if the property has appreciated greatly since it was purchased.

#65. "Reverse mortgages" are an excellent source of cash for any homeowner.

REALITY:

A "reverse mortgage" is a loan which allows senior citizens (62 or older) to convert some of their equity into tax-free income without having to relinquish ownership or make any repayments, as long as there is no existing mortgage balance (or only a very small one), and they continue to live in the home. The cash you get from a reverse mortgage can be paid to you in several different ways: 1) in a lump sum; 2) as a regular monthly cash payment; 3) as a "credit-line" account that lets you decide when and how much of your available cash is paid to you; or 4) in a combination of these methods.

Homeowners may take out reverse mortgages for any number of reasons, from subsidizing their income needs, to traveling around the world. Unlike a regular loan, no reason is needed to be able to "borrow your own money!"

On the plus side, once the lender approves you for a reverse mortgage, there is no requirement for repayment until you sell your residence, move out of it for longer than 12 months, or die. Also, you don't need a minimum income to qualify. Actually, you could have no income at all and still be able to get a reverse mortgage. And, since there are no monthly repayments, there is no possibility of losing your home, as long as you, or any co-owner(s), live in the home. Also, since the money received is in the form of a loan, it is not considered taxable income.

On the negative side, remember that with a reverse mortgage you are taking out cash and increasing your debt. What if your home value decreases? When a reverse mortgage comes due and payable, a lot of money might be owed and there may be little or no equity left in the home (unless your home value has grown considerably). After the loan and fees are repaid, any remaining equity is distributed to you (if you are still alive) or to your estate, for distribution to your heirs. Also, with reverse mortgages, there may be no escrow accounts attached, as may have been the case with a borrower's regular mortgage. Thus, borrowers must remember to accumulate the funds needed to pay taxes and insurance to avoid the risk of foreclosure.

The loan amount for which you are eligible depends upon the age of the youngest titleholder, the amount of equity you have in your home, its appraised value, the then-current interest rate and the fees associated with the loan. There are no income or credit score requirements, but many lenders require homeowners to attend workshops/seminars to fully understand the consequences of reverse mortgages before their application is approved.

The maximum loan amount allowed for your area by the Federal Housing Authority (FHA) also is a critical factor. The limit changes annually and is based upon the area of the country where you live. (More expensive areas such as California and New York have higher limits than South Carolina or Kentucky.) The current limits for each area are available on the Department of Housing and Urban Development (HUD) Website: **https://entp.hud.gov/idapp/html/hicostlook.cfm.**

#66. If I hold title to a property as "joint tenants with rights of survivorship" and if both the joint tenant and I die together, then each of our Wills determines the way our half is distributed.

REALITY

A decedent's Will has no effect on property held in joint tenancy with rights of survivorship. The property automatically goes to the surviving tenant. However, if joint tenants die simultaneously (such as in a plane crash), then the situation is the Will of each joint tenant does indeed determine who receives their share of the property.

However, if the first to die predeceases the other joint tenant by minutes, hours or even a few days, the surviving joint tenant inherits the entire property and, when he or she dies, the property is distributed according to the provisions of his or her Will. The heirs of the first joint tenant get nothing.

#67. The set of federal consumer protection laws that took effect July 30, 2009 does not provide me much added protection.

REALITY

The consumer protection laws that went into effect on July 30, 2009 are directed at consumers who apply for a loan to buy a primary or secondary home, or are planning to refinance their existing mortgage. The law, as spelled out by the Federal Reserve, has several provisions aimed at giving consumers much-needed protections and rights. If the lender does not adhere to these rules, then you have the legal right to walk away without penalty.

First, the new law requires lenders to give you initial disclosures of the cost of your mortgage within three business days of your application. Loan documents must show both the stated interest rate and the annual percentage rate (which takes into account all costs associated with the loan) to allow customers to determine the actual cost of the loan.

Second, except for a small fee associated with checking your credit, the new law prohibits lenders from collecting any fees until the lender has provided you with the required documents. Traditionally, many lenders have collected a whole host of up-front fees amounting to hundreds of dollars at the time of the application.

Third, the new law provides for a seven-day waiting period after you receive the loan disclosure documents mentioned above. You will have up to seven days to think about the transaction and to have "buyer's remorse" before going to closing. Final disclosure documents, along with a copy of the appraisal, are due three business days before the closing. In the past, many lenders did not adhere to this law nor did many borrowers even know it existed.

Fourth, the law also provides for a three-day period after all the loan documents have been signed, in case you change your mind. Disbursement of the funds will not be made until that period has expired.

Fifth, another significant provision of the new law requires lenders to provide you with new disclosure documents if the interest rate on your loan increases by more than one-eighth of a percentage point over the original rate. When this happens, the seven-day waiting period must start over.

All of these provisions are designed to give you, the borrower, much more accurate information before settlement, as well as greater protection than before. The new protections should help minimize settlement "surprises" for you as a borrower.

> **#68. If required by my lender, PMI payments must be paid for the entire life of the loan.**

REALITY

Private Mortgage Insurance (known as "PMI") is insurance usually required by the lender when a homebuyer obtains a loan that is more than 80 percent of the home's value. It is extra coverage for the lender in the event the buyer defaults.

The length of time you must make PMI payments depends upon the type of home loan you have. With a mortgage from a regular financial institution, when you achieve 20 percent equity in your home, many lenders will allow you to cancel PMI if the loan is at least 24 months old, and you have a consistent, timely payment record.

Even with 20 percent equity, it is still almost impossible to get a lender to cancel mortgage insurance payments associated with Federal Housing Authority (FHA) or Department of Veterans Affairs (VA) government-guaranteed loans. In those cases, the only way to get rid of the mortgage insurance is to refinance with a lender who does not require it. With more than 20 percent equity in your home, this should not be difficult, although you will have to incur the cost of refinancing.

In 1998, Congress passed the Homeowner's Protection Act (HPA) which governs the cancellation of PMI payments for loans (excluding FHA or VA loans) obtained on or after July 29, 1999. Under HPA, "...mortgage lenders or servicers must automatically cancel PMI coverage on most loans once you pay down your mortgage to 78 percent of the value, if you are current on your loan." Even if you are not current, the law requires that the lender initiate PMI cancellation proceedings as soon, thereafter, as the loan does become current. HPA requires your mortgage loan servicer to send an annual statement advising you of your rights regarding termination of your PMI.

To figure out whether to refinance or not, you need to know the full price of the new mortgage. This includes total closing costs, pre-payment fees (if any), and the savings, in terms of a lower monthly payment. An analysis of the numbers with and without refinancing should lead you to making the best decision.

A 2007 change in the tax law has been extended that now allows PMI payments to be tax deductible (similar to interest and taxes) on mortgages taken out on first or second homes bought between 2007 and 2010. This tax deduction can be taken for policies issued by private insurers, as well as insurance provided by FHA, VA and the Rural Housing Administration.

The PMI deduction is claimed on Schedule A, Line 13 of your federal tax return, the schedule on which itemized deductions are claimed. Your lender will report to you the amount you paid, annually, in Box 4 of Form 1098. This is the form they send you each year showing the amount of interest and taxes you paid. While there is no limit on the amount of PMI premiums you may deduct, the amount might be reduced depending upon your income.

#69. My wife and I were recently divorced and had been joint owners of the home in which we both lived for more than 10 years. Two years ago, I moved out and my spouse stayed in the home. Last year, the home was sold and generated a substantial gain on the sale which we both will share. I assume I am not eligible for the tax exemption on my portion of the capital gain.

REALITY

Indeed you are entitled to an exemption on your part of the capital gain on the sale of the property. Internal Revenue Code 121 permits a $250,000 capital gains tax exemption to homeowners on the sale of their principal residence in which they lived for 24 out of the 60 months before the sale. Each homeowner is entitled to the exemption.

In this case, since the spouse (your ex-wife) living in the home at the time of sale qualified for the exemption, then so does the spouse (you) who no longer lives in the house. Thus, you each qualify for the exemption up to the $250,000 limit. In addition, most states match their tax laws with the federal tax code so you should be able to claim the exemption on your state tax return as well, if applicable.

#70. If I co-sign on a mortgage for a friend or relative, I will be able to have my name removed from the loan whenever I want.

REALITY

No, no, no! Not true. When you co-sign for a mortgage, the lender uses your credit standing in the decision to grant the mortgage and rarely is willing to let a co-signer off the hook, unless the mortgage is refinanced. The repayment responsibility becomes yours if the primary mortgage holder does not pay.

Your credit rating is at risk, as is that of the other co-signer, for the duration of the mortgage. In the event of default, the lender will likely foreclose on the property and resell it. The lender may sue you if the sale proceeds are insufficient to cover the outstanding balance and the costs associated with the sale. The foreclosure will be reflected on the credit report of both co-signers and will negatively affect your credit rating for years to come. My advice is to think twice before co-signing your good credit away.

#71. Joint tenancy with rights of survivorship (JTWROS) is the "best" way for two people to title property.

REALITY

There are three ways in which two people can jointly hold title:

1. **Tenants In Common**: With this form of ownership, each person owns a specific percentage of interest in the property. While this ownership is usually 50-50, that is not always the case. A property can be owned 60/40, 70/30 or any other combination.

   If one tenant dies, the portion of the property owned by him or her is distributed according to the terms of the decedent's Will rather than automatically to the survivor(s). If there is no Will, then the owner will have died "intestate" and the title to the property must be transferred to the legal heir(s) via probate. Probate is a legal process that takes place after someone's death. It usually involves proving that the deceased's Will is valid, identifying the deceased person's property and having it appraised, paying outstanding debts and taxes, and distributing the property per the Will or state law.

   If there is a Will, after it has been "probated," the deceased's assets will be distributed as specified in the document. If there is no Will, then the assets will be distributed according to the inheritance laws in the jurisdiction where the decedent legally resided. There will be a court-appointed personal representative who will administer the decedent's estate.

If a deed is conveyed without specifying how the title is to be held, the courts will assume the property is titled as "tenants in common." It will be assumed that each tenant owned one half of the property.

2. **Joint Tenants with Rights of Survivorship (JTWROS)**: Both owners equally own an undivided interest in the property. When one of the joint owners dies, the other joint owner automatically becomes the sole owner of the property. There is no requirement for probate. Either joint tenant may assign his interest to a third party, in writing, thus severing the existing joint tenancy. If that occurs, by law, the new ownership relationship between the two tenants then becomes "tenants in common."

3. **Tenancy by the Entireties**: This form of ownership is reserved exclusively for married couples. In this case, husband and wife each own an undivided interest in the property. One big advantage with this form of ownership is, unless both parties owe money to a creditor, the creditor cannot place a lien on the property. Upon the death of one party, the entire property will be owned by the survivor and, again, no probate is necessary.

In reality, there are a variety of ways to hold title to a property. What is "best" depends upon what you are trying to accomplish.

#72. There is no way to terminate a tenant's "life estate" even if the tenant is not taking care of the property and is not paying the property taxes as specified in the "Life Estate Agreement."

REALITY

A "life estate" (i.e., the right to occupy a property for as long as that person lives or until he or she decides to move out) is often provided when you ultimately want to leave a property to another person or institution but first desire to provide someone else a place to live for the rest of his or her life.

For example, you have an adult granddaughter who has lived with and cared for you for years. You want to show your gratitude and ensure that when you die, she still has a place to live. So, in your Will, you give her a "life estate" interest in your house. The Will provides that, upon her death, the house will then go to some other beneficiary such as another family member or a named organization.

If a tenant has a "life estate" and is not living up to the terms of the agreement, you, as the ultimate beneficiary or as the executor of a decedent's Will, may sue that person for waste. The court then decides whether the tenant's violations are so flagrant as to warrant termination of the "life estate." Offering a life tenant a financial incentive to move is often a successful way to get rid of the tenant and to avoid the cost, time and hassle of a legal proceeding.

> **#73. I am ready to send my last check to pay off my mortgage. There is nothing particular I need to know or do before I mail that final check.**

REALITY

Here are a few things you should know and do before making that final payment:

1. Obtain a written payoff statement from your lender or servicer and check it for accuracy.

2. Most states limit the amount of time to no more than 90 days that a lender has to record and return release documents to you. (But, first, follow up with a phone call to make sure your check was actually received. You should receive a confirmation within 30 days.)

3. Once you have confirmed that the lien is off the property and that it has been recorded at the courthouse, you do not need to keep copies of the documentation (since it will be available from the county, if needed). However, I suggest keeping documents showing the amount of interest paid for at least three years, along with other records kept for tax purposes.

4. If you are concerned that you or your lender might miss an important step in the process, you might hire a "settlement agent." In some states, that person has the legal authority to sign and record the "certificate of satisfaction" on the lender's behalf

(but at your expense) if the lender does not do it as timely as you would like. The lender is required, by law, to do it.

So, you can see that actually having the money to pay off the mortgage is only a part of the process. There are a few other steps that you should take to ensure the rest of the process is completed legally.

#74. My friends tell me I am throwing money away by renting when I should be buying my own place. Since I'm very comfortable with things the way they are, there really is nothing further for me to think about.

REALITY

At one time in our history, home ownership was almost a sure path to increased wealth and everybody wanted to be on that course. But once the real estate market turned downward, around 2007, renting became a much more attractive option than it had been. Here are a few reasons:

1. With a real estate market slowdown, there are more potential sellers renting their homes as a way of generating income until the market improves. When this happens, there are more rentals available to you, and owners are offering great deals and incentives to attract renters. Also, many of the newer condos available for rent offer amenities you may not be able to afford in a home such as an exercise facility or a swimming pool.

2. As a renter, you have much more flexibility than you have as a homeowner. If you have to (or just want to) move for any reason

133

such as a job relocation, to find a job, or to be near family and friends, you do not have to go through the tedious process of selling a home before you can move. All you have to do is give notice and remember to adhere to all of your contractual stipulations. You are then free to go.

3. The value of the tax-deductibility of home mortgage interest may be overstated and overrated. While it is indeed a legitimate tax deduction, National Multi Housing Council study results show half of homeowners don't take this deduction because they don't itemize on their tax returns. Even with this deduction, their total deductions do not exceed the amount of the standard federal tax deduction. So, the much-touted deduction goes unused. (For 2009, the standard federal tax deduction is $11,400 for married couples; $8,350 for heads of household; and $5,700 for singles.)

Despite the above, traditionally, home ownership has been considered a hedge against inflation and housing values have risen, over the long-term. Also, owning a home provides you with an asset that increases in value over time as the mortgage is paid down and provides an asset against which you might borrow at a lower rate than an unsecured loan.

Whether to buy or rent is a personal decision that should be made by you, not your friends. Not everyone wants to be a homeowner or is cut out for the responsibilities and hassles of home ownership. You need to examine your own temperament and take a look at several areas of your life, such as your credit history; current debt level; other financial responsibilities; savings; and your income stability. You also need to consider whether you have the money for a down payment and other unexpected household expenses that you do not have to pay as a renter.

If, after evaluating all of these factors, you decide you are ready for home ownership, then, by all means, go for it. Otherwise, wait.

#75. My spouse and I are looking at buying a property that is being represented by a realtor who offered to act as a "dual agent." She says she can get us a better price on the home that way. Can she?

REALITY

A "dual agent" represents both the buyer and seller in a real estate transaction. They are often referred to as "non-agents" because they have no allegiance to either buyer or seller. In some states, "dual agency" is not allowed because it is viewed as unethical. Also, many agencies forbid their agents to work in such a capacity so buyers and sellers can be assured their agent is working for them alone. Using a "dual agent" may result in you paying an inflated amount for the property and possibly not being made aware of property deficiencies.

Why does "dual agency" even exist if it is a questionable practice, and what should you do? It exists because it gives brokers an opportunity to double dip on their own listings. They do not have to split the sales commissions, since they have both sides of the deal. That may work if all parties understand what's going on. However, sometimes, it does not.

There are many pitfalls here and "dual agency" has been the subject of a great number of lawsuits against real estate brokers, resulting in huge damage awards. My suggestion to you is to find an agent who will represent you as the buyer and leave another agent to work for the seller.

135

That's likely to be the way for you to get the best deal and to be assured your interests are being protected.

#76. A fixed-rate mortgage is always better than an adjustable-rate mortgage.

REALITY

Historically, fixed-rate loans have been the loan of choice for most borrowers. That is especially true in a low interest rate environment. But, there are borrowers for whom adjustable-rate mortgages may be appropriate. A professional in the early stages of his or her career, or a person who has limited funds and plans to be in a property for a short period may find that such a loan instrument works for them because of an expectation that their circumstances will change within a short period of time. Thus, even if the rate adjusts upward, they expect to be able to afford the higher payment or, by that time, they expect to have moved.

Adjustable-rate loan payments move up and down as interest rates change, and are tied to an "index." These loan interest rates "adjust" or change at various times, depending upon the contract. For example, contracts usually call for rate changes every 1, 3, 5 or 7 years.

You should find out the index to which your rate is tied. Then, you should look on the web or in the *Wall Street Journal* to see how quickly it has changed, historically. That will help you see how and by how much it moves up and down. Then, determine whether you are comfortable with that amount of fluctuation.

Borrowers who take out adjustable-rate loans must calculate the maximum payment they would have to make under the variable-rate loan structure. Then, they should ask themselves whether they are likely to be able to pay that higher amount should circumstances change and they are forced to remain in the property longer than planned and cannot refinance. If you cannot do this, ask the lender to make the calculation for you before signing the loan documents. Also, you should look at your other financial obligations and the stability of your job situation.

Even though fixed rates are generally higher than adjustable rates, they offer stability, predictability and protection from sticker shock if rates rise.

#77. "No down payment" real estate loans are still readily available for anyone with "good" credit.

REALITY

Given the downturn in the real estate market in the 2000s and the losses many lenders suffered, you are unlikely to find a lender who will make such a loan. (Their memories are not that short.) Since that time, just the opposite has become the norm. Higher down payments of 20 percent or more and higher credit scores of as much as 720 are being demanded by many lenders to get a real estate loan approved at a reasonable rate.

If you don't have the 20 percent to put down on your selected property, my recommendation is that you wait until you have saved that amount and work to ensure your credit record is as clean as possible. The 20 percent downpayment keeps you from having the dreaded private mortgage insurance added to your monthly payment. (See Reality #68.)

#78. There are legitimate firms that can stop my foreclosure.

REALITY

According to the Federal Trade Commission (FTC), foreclosure rescue schemes are "…proliferating across the country as a result of recession-related job losses and the real estate bust." Firms that promise you instant help have no more ability to intervene on your behalf--to work out repayment plans, loan modifications, or short sales with your lender--than you have. What these firms are doing is appealing to your fears and operating out of their own greed. They know you are both fearful and frantic, and might be willing to do anything and pay any amount to get the help you need. To help the public, the FTC has compiled a list of "red flags" to assist homeowners in determining the legitimacy of these firms. They say you should avoid doing business with any firm that:

1. Guarantees to stop your foreclosure regardless of how much you owe or how much you make.

2. Requires an up-front fee before they render any service.

3. Tells you to stop talking with your lender or mortgage servicer directly.

4. Directs you to send mortgage payments to them versus your lender or mortgage servicer.

5. Asks you to sign over the title or deed to your home to them.

6. Promises you they will allow you to "buy back" your home at some point in the future.

"Let the buyer beware!" I advise you to hang up the phone or walk away if you are approached by one of these companies. Remember, as I said in Reality #38, legitimate firms do not advertise on trees, traffic lights and stop signs like many of these illegitimate firms do.

#79. Real estate values have plummeted in my neighborhood to the point that I owe more on my house than its current value. I should just walk away and start over when values come back.

REALITY

When property values fall substantially, large numbers of mortgage holders walk away from properties, especially if they owe more on the house than it is worth. In some cases, homeowners walk away because they have no "skin in the game." That means they have little or nothing invested in the property, or their outstanding balance is so large in comparison to the home's value, they see no reason to continue to make payments.

Before you make the decision to walk away, however, think about the huge hit to your credit score that such abandonment will cause. According to a spokesperson for Fair Isaac Corp., "...A foreclosure is a serious delinquency and is in the same category--as far as credit scores go--as a bankruptcy or tax lien." It will wreak havoc on any credit score by as much as 200 points. A low credit score has many negative implications such as an inability to get a job, the unwillingness of financial institutions to loan you money, and the hesitancy of a landlord to rent to you. So, think twice before you take this drastic step. There may be other options available. You just have to find the one that is right for you.

#80. In the divorce decree, our house was deeded to me. Even though I have paid the mortgage faithfully every month, I cannot claim the mortgage interest deduction because our loan is in my ex-husband's name only. The bank will not even talk to me without his permission. I think this is illegal.

REALITY

The bank is doing nothing illegal. A 1999 privacy law called the Financial Services Modernization Act prohibits a lender from discussing a loan with anyone whose name is not on that particular loan. This is done to protect the privacy of the borrower, so the bank is merely following the law. This problem frequently comes up when couples get divorced or separated, and the loan is in only one of their names.

Since your name is not on the loan, you have no legal responsibility for the loan. It is not your obligation; it is your ex-husband's. Therefore, even though you make the mortgage payments, the IRS will not allow you to claim the interest deduction.

However, there is an exception that might apply in your case. If you have proof you are the beneficial owner of the property, then the IRS might grant you an exception. I suggest you get a letter from your ex authorizing the lender to talk with you, and explain all of this to them. Given this information, they should put the Form 1098 (showing the amount of interest and taxes paid in the current calendar year) in your name. Then, you will be able to take the deductions on your tax return. If this doesn't work, the easiest way to solve this problem is to refinance.

Mimi, Money and Me

CHAPTER 7

INSURANCE

INSURANCE

Mimi-isms:

"Better to be safe than sorry."

"There are only two certainties in life - death and taxes."

"Nobody gets out of this world alive."[5]

#81. I am a healthy 23 year-old woman who has just finished college, am looking for a job and have no health insurance. I've been told to just wait until I find a job and am covered by my new employer's plan.

REALITY

That may not be the great idea you think it is. First of all, not all employers offer health coverage. If they do, coverage may or may not be immediate. Also, when you do become eligible for coverage, you may find it excludes pre-existing conditions. Life is fragile and we never know what might occur. The longer you wait for coverage, the greater your chances of something happening that could make you "uninsurable." It could be an accident or an illness, either of which could result in your having a serious medical (and financial) problem.

As an adult, you are responsible for ensuring your own financial security. Quality health insurance is one of those "must haves." It is a way of protecting your own financial assets.

There is a product called "short term" or "temporary health insurance" that might be worth looking into. This type of health insurance provides coverage for a year or less and is typically purchased by recent college graduates or individuals in between jobs. Short-term health insurance usually provides coverage for surgeries that are required, emergency room visits, hospital care and prescription drugs. Its cost depends upon the specifics of the product purchased. Individuals under the age of 30, who do not smoke, typically pay less than $150 per month for such a policy.

My suggestion is that you at least buy a short-term health insurance policy now to ensure you are covered in the event of an unexpected medical emergency. It can be dropped once you secure employment that offers you a health insurance benefit.

#82. I am a 27-year-old single mother with limited financial resources and need life insurance coverage for myself. I think a whole life policy is better for me than a term policy.

REALITY

The two types of insurance are very different. Let's examine each policy type before making a decision regarding which is best for you.

With term insurance, in exchange for a very reasonable initial premium, you get a guarantee from your insurer to pay your beneficiaries the face amount of the policy at the time of your death. That is the extent of the coverage. Customarily, term life insurance is renewable only up to about age 75 and premiums rise as you get older. However, you can lock in the rates for a certain period of time by buying a 10-, 15- or 20-year "level premium" policy.

On the other hand, whole life insurance not only provides a basic death benefit but also builds up a "cash value" similar to a savings account that you can borrow against or withdraw. Premiums usually remain constant and each payment is divided so that some portion of it pays for the basic coverage and the rest goes into the cash value savings account.

This type of policy usually pays annual dividends that make the cash value account grow. Because some of your premium is going into the savings account, not all of it is available to pay for the pure insurance coverage. Therefore, the cost of an equivalent amount of whole life insurance is going to be much more than the cost of a term policy with the same death benefit.

You purchase life insurance to provide resources for your beneficiaries in the event you are no longer around to provide for them. It seems that, at this point in your financial life, a term policy will give you the best value for your premium dollar. Be sure to shop around and compare the premium amount charged by several insurers for the same amount of coverage. Also, look into the financial stability of each by checking with A.M. Best or Fitch Ratings Insurance Group, both of which are insurance rating agencies. (See Reality #90 for a further discussion of these and other insurance rating companies.)

#83. I am 67 years old and Medicare-eligible. If I need to go into a nursing home, Medicare will cover my stay.

REALITY

Medicare, the nation's largest health insurance program, provides medical care for citizens 65 and older as well as for some under 65 with certain disabilities. However, Medicare does not automatically cover nursing home costs, even for Medicare clients. In fact, Medicare's coverage for nursing home care is quite limited.

Medicare pays only for medically necessary, skilled nursing facility care. Usually, this care is paid for by Medicare for only a short time after a hospitalization (up to 100 days per illness), and only after you have met its very specific requirements. Long-term or custodial care must be paid for out of your own financial resources.

There is another government program, Medicaid, which may provide such coverage, but only after you have exhausted your resources down to the required level (currently about $2,000 in most states). Medicaid has no age limitation and is a health insurance program for those who can't afford to pay for their own care. For qualified clients, it covers care in a nursing home, medical supplies, medical equipment, lab work and X-ray services.

But, be aware Medicaid uses a five-year "look back" rule to determine if and when you become eligible. The "look back" rule examines your resources during the previous five years (it used to be three years until 2008) and makes the eligibility decision as though you still had any resources you may have given away or used up frivolously in order to become eligible for assistance. All transfers, whether to individuals or trusts, are subject to the "look back" rule. This could make the application process more difficult and could result in more applications being denied due to lack of documentation. The "look back" rule clearly is designed to keep people from giving away or spending down their resources and then having the government pick up a tab they easily could have covered themselves.

Here's an example: Let's assume that, as a senior citizen, you transfer $70,000 to your children on July 1, 2006, and keep $100,000 in your name. Let's also assume that you live in a state where the average monthly cost of nursing home care is $7,000. Suppose you had a stroke on July 1, 2007, subsequently moved to a nursing home, and spent down your savings over the following year, leaving you eligible for Medicaid on July 1, 2008, if it weren't for the transfer penalty. After applying the "look back" rule, under the law, you would not be eligible for aid until May 1, 2009. The Medicaid calculation would delay your eligibility for 10 months—the number of months you would have been able to pay for your own care had you not given away $70,000 of your resources.

How your care will be paid for during the intervening 10-months until you become eligible is anyone's guess. However, so you are not left completely on your own, Congress passed a law that requires states to put in place a process for hardship waivers in any case where the implementation of the "look back" rule would result in the patient not being able to get the medical support needed so as not to endanger his or her health. Check with your local Medicaid office for information on your state's policies and practices.

> **#84. I have a big family and lots of friends. Therefore, I don't need long-term-care insurance. That is for people who have no one who can or will take care of them if they get very sick.**

REALITY

Unlike in the old days, in today's more self-absorbed world, there are fewer people willing to take on the responsibility of caring for a sick friend or family member. Long-term-care insurance is designed to help pay an approved assistant or organization to aid you with daily activities you are not able to do by yourself. By purchasing insurance to cover this risk, concerns about how to pay for long-term care should be alleviated.

According to the 2004 MetLife Market Survey of Nursing Homes and Home Care Costs, annual costs for a private room in a nursing home can easily reach $75,000, depending on the region of the country where you live. A 2006 New York Life survey reaffirmed those numbers. (A semi-private room is slightly less.) Medicare is not likely to pick up the tab and Medicaid, if you qualify, may only pick up a portion of the cost. At under $100 per month for most healthy workers between the ages of 25 and 45, the monthly premium for long-term-care insurance is an amount that is affordable. However, premiums do rise the older you are when you purchase the insurance, though, to-date, they have risen only modestly once a policy is purchased.

Most policies allow you to get the care you need either in an assisted living facility or at your home--your choice. Even if you have enough money to pay the substantial cost, having long-term-care insurance is a way of helping you protect your assets. By having insurance, your assets may not have to be liquidated to cover the cost of your care.

In addition, caring for a loved one can take an enormous physical and financial toll on a family. Family members may have to give up their jobs, reduce their employment hours to part-time, dip into their own resources or experience role reversal as a parent becomes the child--often a difficult situation for both.

So, you can see, the size of your circle of friends and family has absolutely no bearing on your need for long-term-care insurance. There are several other factors to consider. My advice is that you purchase a policy that provides for your long-term care should you get sick. **Mimi would say, "Learn to paddle your own canoe."**

#85. I have a teenage son who just got his driver's license. Since he doesn't have a car and would only occasionally drive mine, with permission, my insurance rates should not go up.

REALITY

There are many factors insurance companies use to set your rates. One of the major considerations is the age of licensed drivers in the household. Despite the fact that your son is only an occasional driver and does not have a car of his own, your rates still will be set at a level that reflects the existence of a teenaged, male driver in the home. Therefore, you should expect to see a significant increase in your insurance rates.

#86. I plan to buy a new car that will be the same make and model as my neighbor's. Since we will have the same type of car and live in the same area, I can use her insurance premium as a good estimate of what mine will be.

REALITY

Insurance companies use a number of factors to determine the price of your auto insurance. One factor used is called a "credit-based insurance score" developed by Fair Isaacs Corp., the same folks who developed the FICO credit scoring model. Insurance underwriters use this score to provide an estimate of how likely you are to file a claim that will result in a loss to the insurer. The higher your insurance score, the lower the risk you represent. Historically, when used with other information, insurers have found this score has provided benefits of consistency of application, and better, fairer decisions.

Some of the other elements insurers use to set your premium include:

1. Your driving record (including tickets and accidents)
2. The make, model and age of your car
3. The amount of coverage (and deductible) you want
4. Your claims history
5. Your age (and the ages of all other drivers in the house)
6. The location where the car will be kept
7. Whether or not the car is kept in a garage
8. Whether there is an anti-theft device on the car
9. Whether the car is equipped with air bags

Given the above, you cannot assume your insurance premium will be the same as your neighbor's. It will be set for you based upon the insurer's calculation of the risk associated with your coverage, not hers.

#87. In the event of a burglary, the insurance I pay as a part of my mortgage payment will cover my personal property.

REALITY

Unless otherwise noted, the insurance you pay along with your mortgage payment is fire insurance required by your mortgage holder to protect their investment. It usually does not cover your personal property, such as your big screen television or jewelry. To have such coverage, you must buy either a separate policy that specifically covers personal property or a rider to the fire insurance policy.

#88. My husband and I have separate insurance policies for our cars, and we each pay for our own insurance. This is the most cost-effective way of handling this expense.

REALITY

Having separate policies usually is not the most cost-effective way of handling this expense. The reason is that most insurance companies offer a "multi-car discount" for multiple vehicles on a single policy.

Be sure to compare prices among insurers to determine that you are getting the best value for your money. Compare those of insurers that sell directly with those that sell through agents. Remember, price matters, but so does the level of service provided.

After you make your selection, check with either *Consumer Reports* or a company called J.D. Power and Associates to get a customer satisfaction rating on your selected insurer. Also, check with your state insurance department for information on possible complaints filed against the insurers you are considering.

#89. Vehicle service contracts on new cars are all basically the same.

REALITY

Vehicle service contracts pay for covered repairs after the manufacturer's warranty has expired, and are usually bought from the dealer at the time the car is purchased. However, lately, independent companies have entered this market. The coverage in such contracts varies from one company to the next. It is important for you to look at the contract carefully to see what it does and does not cover, and to choose the options that best fit your needs.

Components a vehicle service contract may include are:

1. Time period (Coverage is for a specific length of time.)

2. Miles driven (Coverage is for a specific number of miles.)

3. Repairs (Coverage may range from specific car components to all mechanical and electrical systems.)

4. Deductible amount (This is the out-of-pocket amount you must pay before the company pays. It can range from $0, meaning no

deductible, to $1,000 or even more. Deductibles may be applied on a "per-visit" basis or to each major system being worked on.)

5. Rental car (This is reimbursement for a rental vehicle during the time your car is being repaired. The amount of time shown in a contract can vary from a few hours up to the entire time the car is in for repair.)

6. Exceptions from coverage (There may be specific things not covered by the contract.)

7. Restrictions regarding where repairs can be or have to be made

8. Whether you must pay first for a service and then get reimbursed or are able to have repairs done on a direct-bill basis to the company with which you have the vehicle service contract.

Given all these variations, you can see there is a lot of work that you need to do before selecting and signing a vehicle service contract. Also, be sure to check with the Better Business Bureau if you are considering a contract with an independent provider.

#90. When trying to decide on which insurance company to use, I don't need to be concerned about the company's financial condition.

REALITY

Yes, you do need to concern yourself with the financial condition of any insurance company with which you are considering doing business. You need to make sure that any company to which you are making premium payments will be around to settle any possible future claims. Insurance policies may span several years or you may pay a lump sum for a "paid-up" policy such as a "20-Year Paid-Up Life Insurance Policy." So, you want to be certain the company is around to provide the benefit you have paid for.

There are several companies that assess insurance companies and rate them. Two of them, A.M. Best and Fitch Ratings Insurance Group, have tracked the insurance industry for decades. More recently, Moody's and Standard & Poor's have begun evaluating insurance companies. They each provide news, up-to-date information about insurance companies, and a five-year rating history. I would highly recommend you look up any insurance company you are considering doing business with before signing on the dotted line. **In other words, to use a Mimi-ism, "Look before you leap."**

#91. It is always a good idea to have collision insurance on any car I drive regularly.

REALITY

Collision insurance covers damages you might cause to a rental, borrowed, or personal vehicle. Most of us keep collision coverage on newer cars but wonder when, or if, we should drop this coverage as our cars age. While there is no set rule for determining whether to keep it or let it go, following are a few considerations:

1. How much is your car worth?

2. How much does the collision coverage cost?

3. What is your collision deductible? When added to the premium, how does this total compare to the car's actual value?

4. If your car is totaled and you have dropped your collision coverage, can you afford the out-of-pocket costs of a rental vehicle until you buy a new vehicle?

5. What services or options would you give up if you drop collision coverage?

6. Do you own your vehicle outright, or is it financed or leased?

As you can see, the choice regarding whether or not to keep collision insurance is driven entirely by your own personal situation.

Collision coverage is not necessarily the only auto insurance coverage you should carry. All states have laws that require the owner/driver of a vehicle to demonstrate the ability to cover the cost of damage they might cause, whether to a person or property.

There is another type of coverage you might consider called "comprehensive" or "other than collision" insurance. A comprehensive policy covers losses to your vehicle and others resulting from incidents not directly related to a collision. For example, comprehensive insurance covers your vehicle if it is stolen; or damaged by flood, fire, wind, hail, animals or from glass breakage. Though comprehensive coverage is not required by most states, if your car is financed or leased, most lien-holders will require it.

In summary, auto insurance is packaged into different insurance coverage types. Make sure you know your state laws regarding mandatory coverage requirements and be certain you adhere to them.

CHAPTER 8

GRAB BAG

GRAB BAG

Mimi-isms

"It's a poor rat that doesn't have but one hole.

"You have to have hope for a better tomorrow."

"Don't look a gift horse in the mouth."

#92. To get more spendable dollars, I can claim enough exemptions to take my federal and state income tax withholdings down to zero and then pay all of my taxes at once when I file my tax return. That way, I can have the full use of my money until it is time to file on April 15th of the next year.

REALITY

The Internal Revenue Service (IRS) and most states operate under a "pay-as-you-go" policy. That means the law requires you to pay your taxes throughout the calendar year and essentially to claim the appropriate number of exemptions on your W-4 Withholding Allowance Certificate so that you will not owe substantial amounts of taxes at the end of the year. Should you end up owing at the end of the tax year, the IRS may calculate the amount of money you should have paid in taxes for each quarter of the year and assess a penalty for under-withholding.

To avoid being assessed an under-withholding penalty, federal law requires that you have on deposit with the IRS, by December 31 of the current tax year, an amount equal to the lesser of 100 percent of the previous year's taxes owed or 90 percent of the current amount owed. If you are a person considered by the IRS to be a "high wage earner," (currently defined as one whose adjusted gross income is more than $150,000) the requirement is that the deposit must be equal to the lesser of 110 percent of the previous year's taxes owed, or 90 percent of the current amount owed.

161

Also, don't forget that if you have NO withholdings, you likely will have to write substantial checks to the federal and, if applicable, state governments, by April 15th. I would not recommend you take this route. Claim the appropriate number of allowances and the correct marital status so, at the end of the year you break even neither owing the IRS or your state, nor getting a huge refund, which only gives the government the interest-free use of your money.

#93. As a senior citizen, I can completely trust my family members to look after my assets.

REALITY

Tread gently. According to the National Center on Elder Abuse, financial swindles are one of the fastest growing forms of domestic elder abuse and rank third on the list of mistreatment of the elderly. In this context, financial swindling or exploitation is defined as the "…illegal or improper use of an elder's funds, property or assets." The National Center reports that adult children are the most frequent abusers of the elderly, with other family members--grandchildren, nieces and nephews--ranking second on the list. It is not financial advisors, strangers or even neighbors who appear to be the largest class of perpetrators of these crimes.

These financial abuses may take on different forms but following are examples of a few you may want to look out for:

Grab Bag

1. A daughter uses your credit card to make personal purchases. (She has the card/number because you gave it to her to pick up your medicine one day.)

2. Your grandson takes one of your checks and makes it out to "cash" or to himself. You actually sign the check because he helps you pay your bills since your eyesight is failing. So, he writes the checks for you and has you sign them. (You just don't know he has written one to himself. He also balances the checking account so you never know the money is gone.)

3. You give a family member Power of Attorney who then uses it to take money out of your investment accounts.

4. A relative pressures you to change your beneficiary designations to him or her on both investment accounts and insurance policies.

5. A nephew tries to con you into putting his name on the title to your house.

6. A relative, who is one of your designated beneficiaries and is being paid to help you, allows your bills to pile up in order to preserve the assets he or she stands to inherit.

7. Sudden offers of help managing your financial affairs come from a distant family member or any other casual acquaintance.

8. A family member suddenly seems to have more money and is driving fancier cars than you know he or she can afford. (Where's the money coming from?)

To prevent financial abuses or at least detect them if they have begun, see the list below to get some ideas of things you can do.

1. Have retirement and Social Security checks direct deposited into your bank account.

2. Monitor your credit card activity.

3. Watch out for charitable donation, credit repair, door-to-door solicitation, work-from-home, telephone solicitation, and get-rich-quick scams.

4. If you are asked to donate to an unfamiliar charity, check them out with your local Better Business Bureau.

5. Resist the pressure to buy anything on the spot.

6. Investigate any get-rich-quick schemes talked about at investment seminars. Again, check with your local Better Business Bureau or research the company on the internet to get further information before giving them money.

7. Ask your financial institution to send duplicate statements to a trusted third party and have that person look at the statements.

8. Establish a relationship with a local elder care attorney who can recognize when a stranger is pressuring you to change your Will or Power of Attorney.

9. As an added protection, many state laws permit a domestic violence victim to keep his/her address confidential through the state's Safe At Home Program. For information, Google "address confidentiality programs" and put in your state's name.

Though we all have heard that elder abuse is on the rise, help is available for victims. Look for the warning signs and tell someone or call for help by dialing the Elder Abuse Hotline at 1-800-752-6200, if you believe you or someone you know needs help.

#94. I can still get ahead, even if I don't set specific goals.

REALITY

Setting goals and working diligently toward them is the surest way I know to achieve those things you say are important to you in life. Again, that old adage is true: "If you don't know where you're going, any road will get you there." Imagine setting out to go "somewhere" but with no particular destination in mind. First, how would you know in which direction to go? Second, how would you know when you arrive? Think about it.

Most goals are either monetary or, at least, have a financial component. For example, I want to buy a new car; I want to go to Paris; I want to learn to play the piano; I want to go back to school. All of these things cost money.

In the world of goal-setting, we talk about making sure that any goals you set are **SMART** goals. **SMART** stands for *S*pecific, *M*easurable, *A*ttainable, *R*ealistic, and *T*ime Bound. **SMART** goals are more likely to be met if you write them down and regularly check your progress toward meeting them. I have heard it said that a goal without a timetable is nothing more than a "dream."

When my spouse and I first got married many years ago, he was a young graduate student and I worked. (Later, we reversed it; I went to graduate school and he worked.) I got paid every Friday. Every Friday after he picked me up from work, like clockwork, we went to the bank and deposited $10 into our joint savings account plus any extra money we were able to save. Our goal was to have a "comma" in our account. We didn't want $999.99; we wanted a "comma." This meant we would have at least $1,000! We were determined to get our "comma" and were motivated to do so. Ultimately, after many months of saving, we got our "comma." We felt this was a **SMART** goal and was one we could (and did) achieve.

Having no financial goals means having no roadmap to where it is you want to go, financially. Goals are not a guarantee. But, I feel certain that without them, the process will be much more difficult.

#95. If I lease a car, I can drive it as many miles as I choose during the lease period, without penalty. Also, insurance and repairs are the leasing company's responsibility, not mine.

REALITY

Neither of these statements is correct. First, most automobile lease contracts have an annual mileage limitation built into them. Typically, this is 12,000 to 15,000 miles per year, unless you pre-pay an extra fee for the privilege of driving more. Should you exceed your contractual limit, then you will be charged a hefty "excess mileage" fee and possibly a charge for "excess wear and tear."

Second, as the driver of the leased automobile, all costs associated with it during the term of your lease are your responsibility. This includes insurance and repairs. In the case of repairs, not only are they your responsibility, but also you must strictly adhere to the schedule outlined in the maintenance booklet. If you do not, it is likely you will be subject to additional charges at the end of the lease.

Here's a real life example of what can happen if you do not pay strict attention to the terms of the lease contract you sign. A participant in one of my classes was very proud of the new Mercedes-Benz he had leased. A single, snappy-looking fellow, he thought his fancy car really enhanced his image with both the ladies and the gents. He said he was so proud of himself and his new car that he drove it everywhere, even places he could have walked. When his lease expired and he went to turn in his car, he was 4,500 miles over his limit! He was charged 45 cents per mile plus additional "excess wear and tear" charges.

So, before you make the decision to lease a car, carefully examine your driving patterns. If you like to drive to visit relatives, have a long daily commute or just like cruising, then leasing might not be for you.

Don't forget, if you lease a vehicle, at the end of the term of the lease, the vehicle belongs to the dealer. To own the car or truck, you then must enter into a purchase contract with the dealer. This usually involves a negotiated purchase price and either paying cash for the vehicle or settling on financing arrangements. In any event, you do not become the rightful owner of the vehicle until you have fully paid for it.

#96. My state's 529 college savings plan is probably the best one for me to set up for my children and grandchildren.

REALITY

The 529 College Savings Plan, created in 1996 and named after the section of the IRS code that authorizes it, is an education savings plan operated by a state or educational institution and is designed to help families set aside funds for future college costs. In a 529 plan, savers put after-tax dollars into an account that typically offers a variety of mutual fund options. Both earnings and distributions are tax-free, as long as they are used for permissible higher education expenses. Investors may invest in any state plan they choose.

Your state may indeed have a good 529 plan, but don't let your search stop there. All 50 states and Washington, D.C. offer 529 college savings plans. So, you should shop around. Before you invest, research several plans, comparing features and benefits.

Though you can invest in the 529 plan of your choice, some states offer tax breaks for their state residents. But, you should take a look at your state plan's fee structure and performance since high fees and lackluster performance can more than undercut any benefit from tax deductions allowed.

In 2008, Morningstar, Inc., a Chicago-based financial information firm, took a close look at the fee structures of various state 529 plans. Based on their fee structures and investment performance, it ranked the following as among the best:

1. Colorado Scholars Choice College Savings Program
2. Illinois' Bright Star College Savings Plan
3. Maryland College Investment Plan
4. Virginia Education Savings Trust and its American Funds

You can make the maximum contribution of $13,000 per-person per year to a 529 plan. Alternatively, you can "front load" your gifts by putting five years' worth of donations in at one time for each person. However, if you do that, then you cannot make another tax-sheltered 529 gift to that individual for another five years.

Understand, there is risk involved in any stock market investment and there is the potential for great gain and significant loss. During the economic downturn and market meltdown of 2008, many 529 plans lost considerable value, seriously impacting some students' college plans, especially those who needed the funds right away.

#97. Is it true that a Series EE U.S. Savings Bond is worth the amount printed on its face?

REALITY:

A Series EE U.S. Savings Bond is issued by the U.S. Treasury Department and is backed by the full faith and credit of the U.S.

government. Its principal and interest never will be lost due to changes in the financial markets.

There are several other reasons people buy these bonds. First, not only are they absolutely safe, but also they can be replaced if lost, destroyed or stolen. Second, you do not have to pay state or local income taxes on the interest they accrue. Third, some Series EE Savings Bonds are federally tax free, if used for education purposes. And, fourth, Series EE bonds never mature, though they stop earning interest after 30 years.

Series EE Bonds are purchased at half the amount shown as their face value. The bond's worth starts out as an amount equal to its purchase price and, over time, with interest, increases to the amount shown as the face value (or more). For example, if you buy a Series EE Savings Bond with a face value of $50, you will pay only $25 for that particular bond. Eventually, its value will rise to $50 (or more). Series EE Bonds continue to earn interest for 30 years and never expire. If held long enough, the value may far exceed the amount shown on the face of the bond. You can go to the U.S. Treasury Department's website at **www.treasurydirect.gov/BC/SBCPrice** and put in the serial number and issue date of your bond to find out its current value.

#98. Using coupons will not save a significant amount of money.

REALITY

Coupons are an incentive by product manufacturers to get you to buy their merchandise. Using manufacturer and store coupons indeed can save you a lot of money as long as you are using them on items you would have bought anyway.

I have an older sister we call the "coupon queen." Everybody in the family knows she loves coupons and uses them extensively. We all save the coupon supplements for her and she proudly collects them from us whenever we visit. She especially likes to combine the use of coupons with other specials such as BOGO (buy one/get one), regularly entertaining us with stories of only paying pennies, or nothing, for items that otherwise would have cost several dollars. She is a true zealot when it comes to coupons. I believe (and think she would agree) she is substantially better off than she would otherwise have been had she not used them so skillfully and so extensively.

Shopping wisely and shopping for bargains just makes good money sense. Frequenting discount stores, watching for store sale ads, and using coupons, all allow you to conserve valuable (and often limited) financial resources that can be used elsewhere or saved. The possibilities are endless.

#99. I am 53 years old and have a 25-year old offspring who won't work and who I am supporting. So, I can't save for my own retirement.

REALITY

Have you ever heard the term "enabler?" This is not a financial term, but, for purposes of this exercise, it certainly has financial implications, especially for you and your financial well-being. In the broad sense of problematic behavior, an enabler makes allowances for a person's bad behavior or habits, thereby perpetuating the harmful conduct. While it is likely the person being enabled will have a difficult time short term, stopping the enabling is the only way to make that person eventually assume responsibility for his or her own actions.

In your case, not only are you crippling your son but also you are failing to take care of your own financial future, especially your retirement. At age 25, your son should be able to support himself. At age 53, you should be well on your way to saving for a comfortable retirement, but you are impeding your own progress by diverting your resources to care for another adult. This is not going to help either of you.

I had a senior federal government manager in one of my classes whose twenty-something son had just graduated from college, tried working for a year, did not like it and was living at home again. She and her husband felt duty-bound to take care of him. They paid for his car, gas, clothes, and entertainment. In short, they covered ALL of his expenses.

Now, he wants to go to graduate school and the parents feel they have to pay for that. When I told her that her son had other options, she looked at me like I had two heads. "What are they?" she exclaimed. I replied that he could get a job; take out a student loan; try to get a scholarship; or just wait until he could afford to pay his own way back to school.

On the other hand, putting money aside for her retirement could not and should not be delayed any longer. I reminded her of the safety briefing given on flights: "In the event of an emergency, an oxygen mask will come down. Put your mask on first." The flight attendant goes on to remind each of us that "…you cannot help anyone else until you have safely secured your own mask."

You should take heed of this message. The best thing you can do for your son, after insisting that he assume responsibility for himself, is to take care of yourself in retirement. You do not want to become the kind of burden on him that he is on you.

#100. Friends tell me there are several ways to avoid the 10 percent early withdrawal penalty on my IRA. I only know of two--disability or death.

REALITY

An IRA "early withdrawal penalty" is a 10 percent fee imposed by the IRS if you withdraw money from a regular IRA for a reason other than those specified in the law, before you are 59 ½ years old and before you have had the money on deposit for at least 5 years.

Besides the two ways of avoiding the 10 percent early withdrawal fee of which you are already aware, there are several other circumstances you may encounter that also will allow the fee to be waived. They are:

1. If you use the money to pay for treatment for an illness or injury that requires expensive medical treatment that exceeds 7.5 percent of your adjusted gross income
2. If you pay for higher education expenses for yourself, your spouse, your children or grandchildren

3. If you use the money withdrawn to pay back taxes owed to the IRS after the IRS has placed a levy against your IRA

4. If you are a first-time homebuyer (up to a maximum of $10,000)

Remember, although you may avoid the penalty, if any of the qualifying events listed above occurs, you should make every effort to avoid taking money out of your IRA early. Not only will you have to pay taxes immediately, but also you will be losing many years of tax-free compounding that could cost you thousands of dollars.

#101. I am a 61-year old divorced female who was a stay-at-home spouse for 25 years. When I am eligible for Social Security, I'm afraid I may not get any credit for the 25 years I spent at home.

REALITY

Since you were married for more than 10 years, you can get a Social Security benefit based on your ex-husband's employment record, even if he has remarried. At most, your benefit will be equal to half of his full-retirement-age monthly benefit. For example, if he is entitled to receive $2,000 a month at full-retirement age, then you will be eligible to receive a $1,000 monthly benefit at your own full-retirement age if this amount is larger than what you could get based on your own work record.

There are a few other eligibility requirements that must be met before your benefits can begin. One, your ex-husband must be at least 62 years old and must be eligible for or receiving Social Security benefits. Two, you must be at least 62 years old. (If your ex-husband is deceased, you may be eligible at age 60.) And, three, you must be unmarried. If your ex-spouse has not applied for retirement benefits but can qualify for them, you still may apply, as long as you meet the other criteria and have been divorced for at least two years.

If you re-marry, generally, you cannot collect benefits on your ex's employment record unless your later marriage has ended. However, if you re-marry after age 60 and your ex dies, then you can qualify for a widow's benefit, based on your ex's work history.

Just as is the case with regular Social Security benefits, you may start receiving this benefit at age 62, but you will receive a reduced amount. In any event, the amount of benefits you get has no impact on the amount of benefits your ex-husband or his current wife gets.

If your former spouse is deceased and you need information about survivor's benefits, the Social Security Administration (SSA) has published two booklets you may find helpful. One is, "If You're the Worker's Surviving Divorced Spouse." The other is, "What Every Woman Should Know," which discusses issues related to divorce, remarriage, and widow's benefits. SSA can be reached either by calling 1-800-772-1213 or by going onto their website at **www.socialsecurity.gov/pubs**.

Mimi, Money and Me

Appendix A

CREDIT SCORE DESCRIPTION AND RELATED TIPS

The FICO score, the credit score used most frequently by lenders, is based on the five components listed below. FICO scores range from 300 to 850. The higher the score, the more creditworthy you are. Also, the higher your credit score, the lower the risk and, therefore, the lower the cost of credit you likely will have to pay.

The FICO score components and the relative weight each contributes to your overall score are as follows:

1. Your payment history--how timely you've been with payments. **35%**
2. Your current total debt--how much you owe compared with your total available credit. **30%**
3. Length of your credit history--how long a credit history you have. **15%**
4. Types of credit you have outstanding--what mix of credit types you have. **10%**
5. Your requests for new credit--whether you've recently taken on new credit or debt. **10%**

Here are a few credit score-related tips:

1. According to Zogby International, one of the country's largest public opinion pollsters, a third of people who have pulled their credit reports have found errors in them. So, be sure to get a copy of your report from each credit bureau and read it! Getting an error fixed can raise your score by as much as 200 points, according to John Ulzheimer, president of consumer education at **www.Credit.com**.

2. Paying your bills on time is the single most important contributor to a good credit score. "Even one late payment can reduce a 750-plus credit score by 100 points," according to Mr. Ulzheimer,

".....but, if you catch up within 30 days, you may be able to get back on track." CNN reports that a payment that's more than 90 days late can cause damage to your credit score for years.

3. If you feel you want to cancel some of your credit cards, don't cancel your oldest cards since 15% of your credit score is determined by the length of your credit history.

4. According to *Money Magazine*, "...mortgage and car loan inquiries made within the most recent 30 days are not figured into the credit score calculation. Any inquiries within a 14-day period before that count as one inquiry."

5. Pay off debt rather than move it around. Creditors can easily tell that an old balance has been "paid off" while a new account has been opened with an almost identical balance. They are not fooled.

Your FICO score makes a huge difference in the way lenders view you and, consequently, the rate a potential lender is likely to charge you. So, know your score; correct any errors found on your credit report; and manage your score carefully.

For more information on credit scores and credit reports, go to the FICO website located at **www.myfico.com/CreditEducation.** (See Appendix B for contact information for the three major credit bureaus--Equifax, Experian and TransUnion.)

Appendix B
Helpful Resources

- **Financial Websites**:
  - a) Rich Dad/Poor Dad: **www.richdad.com**
  - b) Social Security Administration: **www.ssa.gov**
  - c) Teaching kids about money: **www2.cibc.com/smartsmart/parent/TeachingThemAbout Money.html**
  - d) Shows kids, teens and adults how to get on the road to financial freedom: **www.creativewealthintl.org**
  - e) Provides information on credit, budgets, automobile financing, mortgages, banking and insurance: **www.SmartEdgeByGMAC.com**
  - f) Fidelity Investments: **www.fidelity.com**
  - g) Charles Schwab Investments: **www.schwab.com**
  - h) Life Insurance: **www.usaa.com; www.quotesmith.com**
  - i) Disability Insurance: **www.mutualofomaha.com; www.aetna.com; www.diexpert.com; www.statefarm.com; www.northwesternmutual.com**
  - j) Long-term-care Insurance: **www.gefn.com; www.jhancock.com; www.ltcinsurance.com**

- **Books**:
  - a) *Rich Dad, Poor Dad*, Robert Kiyosaki
  - b) *Personal Finance for Dummies*, Eric Dyson
  - c) *The Money Book – A Smart Kid's Guide to Savvy Saving and Spending*, Elaine Wyatt and Stan Hinden
  - d) *In the Black: The African-American Parent's Guide to Raising Financially Responsible Children*, Fran Harris
  - e) *Smart Couples Finish Rich*, David Bach
  - f) *7 Money Mantras For A Richer Life*, Michelle Singletary
  - g) *The Road to Wealth*, Suze Orman
  - h) *The Ultimate Allowance Book*, Elisabeth Donati

- **Credit Reporting Agencies**:
    - a) **Equifax:**
      P.O. Box 740241
      Atlanta, GA 30374
      1-800-685-1111
      www.equifax.com

    - b) **Experian:**
      P.O. Box 2002
      Allen, Texas 75013
      1-888-567-8688
      www.Experian.com

    - c) **TransUnion Corporation:**
      P.O. Box 390
      Chester, PA 19022
      1-800-916-8800
      www.transunion.com

- **Other**:
    - a) **Federal Trade Commission**
      CRC-240
      Washington, D.C. 20580
      www.ftc.gov
      You can write to this agency if documented evidence of an error is not acted upon by each credit bureau within 30 days. They also enforce credit laws and provide free information.

    - b) **Fair Credit Reporting Act**
      1-877-382-4357
      www.ftc.gov/os/ststutes/frca.html
      This act gives you the right to know what information is being distributed about you by credit reporting agencies.

c) **National Foundation for Credit Counseling –**
   www.nfcc.org
   This foundation will help you find a professional non-profit credit counseling service.

d) **Consumer Credit Counseling Service**
   www.cccsf.org
   This service will advise you how to clear up a bad credit report.

e) **Department of Housing and Urban Development**
   www.hud.gov
   HUD provides information about home financing.

f) **Department of Veterans Affairs**
   www.homeloansva.gov
   VA provides home financing information for veterans.

g) **HUD/FHA**
   www.hud.gov/fha/loans/cfm
   Contact this organization for information on FHA loans.

h) **A.M. Best Rating Agency**
   www.ambest.com
   Contact this agency for insurance company ratings and to determine their financial soundness.

i) **NAIC**
   www.naic.org/state_web_map.htm
   This site provides information on the licensing status of an insurance company.
   For an insurance company's complaint history, go to:
   www.naic.org/cis/index.do

j) **FICO**
   www.myfico.com
   Provides information about credit reports.

k) **GMAC Financial Services**
1-800-327-6278
www.SmartEdgeByGMAC.com
This site provides educational information on credit and budgeting; automobile financing; mortgages; and banking and insurance.

l) **Websites for Kids**:
www.kidsenseonline.com; www.finishrich.com; www.coolbank.com; www.kidsource.com; www.bigchange.com; www.kipplinger.com/kids

m) **Financial Planners:**
1-800-322-4237
www.fpanet.com
This site allows you to search for names of certified financial planners, by zip code.

Appendix C

Creating a Budget - How Do You Do It?

A budget is simply an "at-a-glance look" at **ALL** of your expected income and expenses over a given period of time. The period covered should be for at least three months, but six months or more is preferred since that gives you a better picture.

Making a budget requires a bit of patience but, if done accurately, it will help you determine whether you can afford the lifestyle you want to live. Following are the steps you need to take.

1. Gather all of the documentation you have showing your income and expenses over the last six months. You will need items such as:
    a) Check registers
    b) Bank statements
    c) Credit card statements
    d) Bill stubs for expenses such as utilities, rent/mortgage, childcare, repairs, insurance and medical expenses
    e) Car payment book
    f) Mortgage or rent statements
    g) Pay stubs
    h) Tax returns
    i) Other, such as tip records, gifts, etc.

2. Make a separate pile containing the receipts/documentation for each expense category. This includes items such as:
    a) Housing, including taxes and insurance
    b) Transportation, including car payment, repairs and maintenance, gasoline, tags, insurance, road service, parking, and vehicle personal property taxes, if applicable
    c) House maintenance
    d) Food

    e) Utilities, including electricity, gas, water, alarm monitoring, phones (cell and land lines), cable, trash and water

    f) Entertainment

    g) Vacation/travel

    h) Laundry

    i) Savings--regular, retirement, and emergency

    j) Contributions/Tithes

    k) Homeowner association fees, where applicable

    l) Medical, including co-pays and prescriptions

    m) Insurance statements, including disability, life, and long-term care

    n) Personal items, including hair and nails

    o) Gifts, including Christmas, birthdays, anniversary, etc.

    p) Clothing

    q) Outstanding debts, including student loans, existing credit cards

    r) Estimated federal and state taxes (if needed)

    s) Allowance

    t) Miscellaneous

3.   Add up the receipts for each expense category and divide by the number of months of receipts you have. (This gives you your average monthly expense, by type.)

4.   Make a listing of all of your income sources, by month, including beginning checking account balance, net salaries, retirement income, child support, alimony, gifts, and any other income.

5.   In a table, similar to the sample shown following these instructions, list all of the income and expenses from the steps above, in the appropriate months. By the time this is complete, essentially every dime of income and expenses you expect to receive or pay should be reflected in the table.

6.   Add up all of your income, by month; then add up all of your expenses, by month.

7. Subtract expenses from income, by month. (Some months will be positive; some will be negative.)

8. Add together all the monthly positives and negatives. If this total is negative, either find other sources of income or reduce expenses to make sure the total of the positives and negatives is zero or a positive number. This will ensure your budget reflects a lifestyle you can afford.

Even after you have completed making your budget for the chosen period, a budget is not fixed forever. You must perform regular reviews and make changes to it as life circumstances change.

Changes to the budget may be required when there are new events such as:

1. Salary adjustments
2. New tax schedules
3. New family goals
4. A change in family status--marriage, divorce, separation
5. New family members

Remember, a budget is not meant to shackle you. Instead, if done so that it accurately and completely reflects your and your family's income and expenses, it can be your ticket to financial freedom.

Mimi, Money and Me

Budget Spreadsheet
Page 1

RESOURCES & EXPENSES \ MONTH	JUL	AUG	SEP	OCT	NOV	DEC	TOTALS
CASH ON HAND	65						65
CHECKING ACCT BAL	375						375
CHECKS FOR DEPOSIT							0
CHG ACCT CREDITS							0
MONIES OWED TO YOU	25						25
SALARY (IES)							
YOU	2,500	2,500	2,500	2,500	2,500	2,500	15,000
YOUR SPOUSE	1,850	1,850	1,850	1,850	1,850	1,850	11,100
TAX REFUND				300			300
GIFTS	25	25	25	25	25	500	625
INTEREST / DIVIDENDS	12						12
OTHER							0
TOTAL RESOURCES	4,852	4,375	4,375	4,675	4,375	4,850	**27,502**

186

RESOURCES & EXPENSES \ MONTH	JUL	AUG	SEP	OCT	NOV	DEC	TOTALS
WITHHOLDINGS--YOU:							
TAXES/ BENEFITS	800	800	800	800	800	800	4,800
401(K) PLAN	75	75	75	75	75	75	450
OTHER	12	12	12	12	12	12	72
WITHHOLDINGS--SPOUSE:							
TAXES/ BENEFITS	662	662	662	662	662	662	3,972
401(K) PLAN							0
OTHER	6	6	6	6	6	6	36
DONATIONS	20	20	20	30	20	30	140
SAVINGS	200	200	200	200	200	200	1,200
HOUSING:							
1ST MORTGAGE	917	917	917	917	917	917	5,502
2ND MORTGAGE							0
TAXES & INSURANCE	175	175	175	175	175	175	1,050
MAINTENANCE	50	50	50	50	50	50	300
LAWN CARE							0
FURNISHINGS / APPLIANCES					250		250
UTILITIES:							
GAS							0
ELECTRICITY	65	65	65	80	100	125	500
WATER	53		55		45		153
BURGLAR ALARM							0
CABLE	30	30	30	30	30	30	180
PHONE SERVICES:							
HOUSE PHONE	20	20	20	20	20	20	120
MOBILE PHONES	40	40	40	40	40	40	240
INTERNET ACCESS							0
NEWSPAPER							0
INSURANCE:							
AUTO	100	100	100	100	100	100	600
MEDICAL PRESCRIPTIONS/CO-PAY	25	25	25	25	25	25	150
LIFE							0
LONG-TERM CARE							0

187

Mimi, Money and Me

Budget Spreadsheet
Page 3

RESOURCES & EXPENSES \ MONTH	JUL	AUG	SEP	OCT	NOV	DEC	TOTALS
AUTO- RELATED EXP:							
CAR PAYMENT	155	155	155	155	155	155	930
TAGS / LICENSE			90				90
ROAD SERVICE					47		47
REPAIRS		100			200		300
GASOLINE	120	120	120	120	120	120	720
PARKING							0
CONSUMER LOANS:							
CREDIT UNION	60	60	60	60	60	60	360
VISA	125	125	125	125	125	125	750
EDUCATIONAL							0
CHILDCARE	200	200	200	200	200	200	1,200
FOOD	225	225	225	225	225	225	1,350
CLOTHING	25	25	25	25	25	25	150
LAUNDRY/SHOE REPAIR	15	15	15	15	15	15	90
HAIR / HAIR PRODUCTS	25	25	80	25	25	80	260
TUITION							0
TRANSPORTATION	10	10	10	10	10	10	60
ENTERTAINMENT	25	50	25	25	50	25	200
VACATION (S)							0
GIFTS:							
BIRTHDAYS		50			50		100
CHRISTMAS						500	500
OTHER							0
ALLOWANCE:							
YOU	40	40	40	40	40	40	240
YOUR SPOUSE	40	40	40	40	40	40	240
MANICURIST							0
OTHER	50	50	50	50	50	50	300
TOTAL EXPENSES	4,313	4,437	4,512	4,337	4,964	4,937	27,502
MONTHLY PLUS/MINUS	537	-62	-137	338	-589	-87	0
CUMULATIVE BAL	537	475	338	676	87	0	

188

Appendix D

Sample Computation of Retirement Income Funding Needs

Assumptions:
1. You have budgeted for retirement expenses of $80,000 per year, in today's dollars.
2. You expect to work another 20 years and to continue to save for retirement.
3. You expect to receive $70,000 pension and Social Security income, at retirement.
4. You have already saved $75,000 toward your retirement.
5. You have a retirement fund valued at $65,000, today.
6. You anticipate a return on investment of 5% per year and a 3% inflation rate.
7. You anticipate you will live 25 years in retirement.

Computation:

1. Amount required to duplicate purchasing power of $80,000 at 3% inflation 20 years from now (when you retire).	$144,489
2. Minus projected annual Social Security/pension payments	-$70,000
3. Remaining annual income target to be funded	$74,489
4. Capital required to produce $74,489 annually at 5% for 25 years	$1,049,844
5. Minus value of current capital assets of $75,000 at 5% for 20 years (until retirement)	-$198,997
6. Minus value of retirement funds of $65,000 at 5% for 20 years (until retirement)	-$172,464
7. Additional capital required by retirement in 20 years	$678,383
8. Annual savings required to be put aside at 5% per year for 20 years (until retirement)	$20,516
9. Monthly savings required to be put aside at 5% per year for 20 years (until retirement)	$1,650
10. Bi-weekly savings required to be put aside at 5% per year for 20 years (until retirement)	$760

Note: For automated retirement income planning calculation tools, google "retirement income calculations" and input your particular parameters.

Appendix E
More Mimi-isms

1. You make one step; I'll help you make two.
2. A man can't ride your back unless it's bent.
3. Where there's a will, there's a way.
4. One good turn deserves another.
5. A picture is worth a thousand words. [6]
6. A place for everything and everything in its place.[7]
7. When you bat an eye, you lose sight of the world.
8. What you don't know won't hurt you.
9. A bird in the hand is worth two in the bush.[8]
10. Some people look at a donut and see the donut; others look at a donut and see the hole.
11. Laugh and the world laughs with you; cry and you cry alone.
12. Don't bite the hand that feeds you.
13. I may not agree with what you say, but I'll defend 'til death your right to say it.
14. Every goodbye is not gone; every shut eye is not asleep.
15. As children, they are tied to your apron strings; as adults, they are tied to your heart strings.
16. The Lord helps those who help themselves.
17. It's always darkest before the dawn.
18. Never trouble trouble 'til trouble troubles you.
19. As long as there's life, there's hope.
20. It's a poor rule that only works one way.
21. You can pick your friends, but you can't pick your relatives.
22. There's a time and; place for everything.
23. The sun's gonna' shine in my backyard someday.
24. No man is an island.
25. Such is Life

---

[6] Frederick Barnard; early 20th century
[7] Ben Franklin, Samuel Smiles
[8] Compleat British Songster, 1781

Index

Index

CPSIA information can be obtained at www.ICGtesting.com
Printed in the USA
BVOW030720121211

278112BV00007B/2/P